## DATE DUE

| | | |
|---|---|---|
| NO 17 '97 | | |
| ~~JE 21 07~~ | | |
| DE 2 08 | | |
| DE 1 9 08 | | |
| MY 2 8 '19 | | |
| JE 1 8 '19 | | |
| | | |
| | | |
| | | |
| | | |
| | | |
| | | |
| | | |
| | | |

DEMCO 38-296

# BUSINESS AND SOCIAL ETIQUETTE WITH DISABLED PEOPLE

## A Guide to Getting Along with Persons Who Have Impairments of Mobility, Vision, Hearing, or Speech

*By*

### CHALDA MALOFF, PH.D.

*and*

### SUSAN MACDUFF WOOD, M.A.

*Foreword by*

**Mel Tillis**

# CHARLES C THOMAS • PUBLISHER
*Springfield • Illinois • U.S.A.*

*d Throughout the World by*

MAS • PUBLISHER
First Street
Illinois 62717

© *1988 by* CHARLES C THOMAS • PUBLISHER
ISBN 0-398-05463-0 (cloth)
ISBN 0-398-06266-8 (paper)
Library of Congress Catalog Card Number: 88-2134

With THOMAS BOOKS *careful attention is given to all details of manufacturing
and design. It is the Publisher's desire to present books that are satisfactory as to their
physical qualities and artistic possibilities and appropriate for their particular use.*
THOMAS BOOKS *will be true to those laws of quality that assure a good name
and good will.*

*Printed in the United States of America*
SC-R-3

**Library of Congress Cataloging-in-Publication Data**

Maloff, Chalda, 1946–
    Business and social etiquette with disabled people.

    Includes index.
    1. Physically handicapped.   2. Physically handicapped—
Public opinion.   3. Etiquette.   4. Business etiquette.
5. Physically handicapped—Conduct of life.   I. Wood,
Susan Macduff.   II. Title.
HV3011.M23   1988        395'.0880816        88-2134
ISBN 0-398-05463-0.— ISBN 0-398-06266-8 (pbk.)

# THIS BOOK HAS BEEN ENDORSED BY

*Business and Social Etiquette with Disabled People* is an impressive manuscript and an imaginative and concrete way to deal with attitudes. The AFB certainly endorses it.

*American Foundation for the Blind, Inc.*

At long last! A well written and precise publication that should be read by every able-bodied American.

*American Amputee Foundation, Inc.*

. . . This book is greatly needed, and you have done a good job with it.

*Raymond Burr, Actor*

This book is important because it can quicken the sensitivities of the majority community. It can be a catalyst for improving public understanding and acceptance of disabled people.

*National Organization on Disability*

We are pleased to endorse . . . your book. We are confident it will make thousands of business, social, and casual contacts between sighted and blind people more comfortable and enjoyable for both.

*American Council of the Blind*

I know I speak for the visually impaired at large when I say, "Thank you for dealing with this matter so thoroughly."

*George Shearing, Musician*

I felt very positive after reading the book . . . I can give you my personal endorsement.

*Robert R. Davila, President*
*Conference of Educational Administrators Serving the Deaf, Inc.*

Hearing loss is a major communication barrier affecting nearly 10 percent of the total American population . . . The authors . . . have done an excellent job in compiling a series of common sense "rules" for improving verbal exchanges.

*Marjorie A. Boone, Member of the Board of Directors*
*Self Help for Hard of Hearing People*

I am sure that your manual will have a positive impact on the way the visually impaired population will be viewed . . . in the future.

*Ronald L. Miller, Ph.D., Executive Director*
*Blinded Veterans Association*

It is a pleasure to endorse such a book.

*Board for Evaluation of Interpreters, Texas Commission for the Deaf*

Those of us trying to educate the public . . . can relax a bit. Your book will meet many needs and calm many fears.

*Disability Focus, Inc.*

... This book should be a welcome addition to public and college libraries ... This should be required reading for those considering a career working with the disabled.

*National Fraternal Society of the Deaf*

You will find yourself saying, "I never thought of that," over and over again.

*National Stuttering Project*

The material reflects sensitive insight ... Employers and others among the general population should find this ... helpful in facilitating communication with hearing-impaired persons.

*Merv Garretson*
*Special Assistant to the President, Gallaudet University*
*Former President, National Association of the Deaf*
*Member of the Board of Directors, World Federation of the Deaf*

... A helpful guide for all who may have contact with disabled citizens.

*The Polio Information Center*

... This is to confirm endorsement by our association ... On a personal level, I ... wished I had a copy many years ago.

*Carl D. Brininstool, on behalf of the*
*Texas Association of the Deaf*

... Many of the topics covered are extremely relevant to professionals dealing with seniors ...

*National Association of Independent Living Centers*

... You have performed a valuable service to able-bodied people as well as to people with disabilities.

*Dr. William E. Castle, Director*
*National Technical Institute for the Deaf*

... I would not hesitate to recommend it to friends, relatives (of hearing-impaired people), and really, to ... everyone.

*Don D. Roose, ACSW, National Executive Director*
*Registry of Interpreters for the Deaf, Inc.*

... This book will be an important contribution to the general public's comprehension of and reaction to handicaps ...

*National Association for Spastic Dysphonia*

This book contains many helpful hints for communicating with hard of hearing and deaf people.

*Alexander Graham Bell Association for the Deaf, Inc.*

## THIS BOOK HAS BEEN RECOMMENDED BY

It is time for all of us to look beyond the disability to the person, and this book . . . helps us to do that . . . the National Easter Seal Society is pleased to recommend it.

*National Easter Seal Society*

*To Jean and Ralph Macduff*

*and*

*To Lisa Maloff and Slava Braun*

# FOREWORD

There was a time when a physical impairment was something to be hidden away and not discussed. Happily, things have changed. Public buildings have ramps for wheelchairs, the morning news program has an interpreter for the deaf, and advertisers hire me, a stutterer, to increase their sales of hamburgers!

While we have come a long way, we have farther to go. The right kind of information about impairments is not yet reaching enough people, and misconceptions continue to exist. Some people shy away from those of us with disabilities because they are uncomfortable with the unknown.

Strangers have mistaken my stutter for evidence of intoxication and have shunned me on street corners. Acquaintances have said, "Why don't you just sing all the time?" as if that would solve my problem. My friends in wheelchairs and with other disabilities agree with me: a little understanding about impairments would go a long way.

I believe most people are well-meaning. They simply lack the good information they need to be able to deal realistically with physical impairments. Hopefully, this book will be a step in the right direction.

Mel Tillis

# PREFACE

The hardest part about writing this book was choosing the title.

We hesitated to use the term "disabled people," since this phrase implies a well-defined group, set apart from the rest of the world. That concept is, of course, inaccurate. The corollary to the old maxim, "No one gets out of this alive," is that virtually everyone, at some point in life, experiences a physical impairment.

Also the word "etiquette" did not quite hit the mark, since nowhere in this book do we give information which will save the reader from someday getting a fish course and discovering he has already used his fish fork. Many of the traditional rules of etiquette are of little consequence in the large scheme of things, and we feel the issues we address here are definitely consequential. How we are treated by those around us determines, in large part, the quality of our lives.

On the positive side, the title we selected is generally descriptive of our topic. And, unlike the majority of the candidates we came up with, it fits nicely on a book jacket without requiring a microdot.

We gathered the information for this book by talking with hundreds of experts on the topic—people who had lived with some kind of physical impairment for at least three years. These people were men and women, young and old. Most were employed; others were retired, homemaking, or attending college. Some had both public and private lives; we have honored the anonymity we promised them.

The many quotations throughout the book were contributed by these people, orally, in writing, or in sign language. The humor and perspective they brought to this project were truly irreplaceable.

These people gave of their time and energy because they believed their personal lives, and the lives of others, would be enhanced by the availability of this book. We hope their faith in our project proves well placed. We hope that businesses and government agencies will take advantage of our information to strengthen their relations with the people they serve and employ. We hope that members of the health care professions will extend the good they do by considering our feedback from their patients. We hope that social, professional, and family relationships will improve once awkwardness and uncertainty about disabilities are replaced with familiarity and understanding.

This book focuses on three groups of disabilities, although we realize there are others. *Section One* deals with mobility impairments, those impairments which affect a person's ability to move around and perform tasks. *Section Two* addresses blindness and the many other types of visual impairments. *Section Three* concerns those impairments affecting the ability to hear or speak. We formulated our recommendations to be broadly applicable, recognizing that no two impairments are exactly alike.

We anticipate that many readers will use this book as a quick reference, reading only the parts which apply to a particular circumstance at a given time. However, we suggest that those who want a fuller understanding of a type of impairment read the entire pertinent section.

The people who kindly reviewed early versions of our manuscript had more questions on our choice of pronouns than on any other single issue. To lay the matter to rest: these choices were purely arbitrary. English having no neuter pronoun, we decided, at random, to refer to mobility-impaired people and communication-impaired people with the masculine pronoun, visually impaired people with the feminine. Nondisabled people in the book were assigned their gender on a first come, first served basis.

While we researched this book extensively, and while one of us has had a physical impairment for many years, we do not presume to speak for all disabled people. We acknowledge that some will disagree with our positions. We offer straightforward, tangible suggestions, and we encourage our readers to freely adapt our advice to the individuals and situations they encounter.

Although this book is intended primarily for nondisabled people, we have found people who are physically impaired to be understandably interested in our topic. To our disabled readers: we welcome your additional ideas, and we are anxious to hear from you!

# ACKNOWLEDGMENTS

We extend our heartfelt thanks to the many physically impaired people who believed in this book and who took the time from their busy schedules to talk with us about their social and business relationships. Their willingness to speak candidly about their personal lives made this book possible. We appreciate their generosity more than we can say.

We are also grateful to many others who encouraged us along the way and helped to make this project a reality. Ms. Kathy Donoho, formerly of the Houston Center for Independent Living, Ms. Vicki Sorrells Harris of the Houston Center for Independent Living, and Mr. C. Donald Rossi were particularly supportive of the work which focuses upon mobility impairments. Ms. Shirley Kopecky assisted in the distribution of questionnaires among mobility-impaired respondents. Dr. Keith Burau and Dr. Margaret A. Nosek provided critical review of the mobility-impairment section. Mrs. Barbara Schneidler and Mrs. Sherri Nance of The Lighthouse of Houston, Ms. Kay Bryant of the Taping for the Blind, Inc., and Ms. Nadine Saffell of the Houston Council of the Blind provided assistance for the section which focuses on visual impairments. Ms. Nadine Saffell and Ms. Sherry Fogg offered critical review of this section. Ms. Carolyn McCaskill Emerson and Mr. Charles D. Trevino of the Houston Community College, Mr. Charles Cooper of MobileComm, Ms. Linda Hall, formerly of Hear-Say, Mr. John Ahlbach of the National Stuttering Project, and Dr. Thomas A. Crowe of the National Association of Voice Disorders were particularly helpful in assisting with the research for the section which focuses on communication impairments. Ms. Deborah Gunter served as a signing interpreter for many interviews. Ms. Gloria Rubenstein, Ms. Victoria Benson, Ms. Michelle Bailey, and Ms. Kathy Weldon provided critical review of this section.

We owe special thanks to Ms. Sandy Sheehy, for her optimism and encouragement when all paths looked bleak, and Dr. Mark Schied of the Department of English, Rice University, for his initial review of the manuscript. Finally, our deepest appreciation goes to Russell Zears and Ralph Wood, whose patience and support have been paramount in the completion of this work.

# CONTENTS

# BUSINESS AND SOCIAL ETIQUETTE
## WITH
## DISABLED PEOPLE

**Section One**

# ETIQUETTE WITH MOBILITY-IMPAIRED PEOPLE

# 1.

## SOME PRELIMINARIES

I came to work badly sunburned one day, and a colleague said, "You look like you've been waterskiing or something." She immediately laughed and felt foolish because I can't use my legs and obviously don't waterski. I appreciated the humor in the situation, but more than that, I took pleasure in knowing that she no longer thought of me as a "disabled" person, but simply as a person.

Almost everyone has experienced an impairment of strength, muscle control, or range of motion. Such impairments, which affect the ability to move around or perform physical tasks, can be called "mobility impairments."

Each mobility impairment is unique. Some are apparent to the casual observer, others are not.

I can't move my arms at all, a fact that isn't obvious from looking at me. New acquaintances often extend an arm for a handshake, and they are taken aback when I don't follow suit. There's always a moment of bewilderment before I can explain.

For people who have long-term mobility impairments, creative solutions are a way of life. Ingenuity takes the place of brute force in many of the tasks of living.

Since I don't walk well, people are always surprised to learn that I cut my own lawn. I have a wheelchair with a motor on it, and I just attach the lawn mower to the wheelchair and go.

A mobility impairment can affect only one part of the body or several. It can be temporary or lasting. It can be substantial, or it can be so slight that it hardly matters in daily life. It can be fairly constant in character, or it can fluctuate over time. In some cases, certain appliances can be used to enhance physical abilities, such as wheelchairs, crutches, walkers, canes, or artificial limbs.

Given the diversity of mobility impairments, compiling some pertinent rules of etiquette might seem like a losing proposition. But, in fact, certain basic principles are broadly applicable. The recommendations in

5

this section will help the reader gracefully deal with the outward mechanics of life so that these do not interfere with the more meaningful aspects of personal relationships.

# 2.

## PRACTICALITIES

### When to Lend Aid

Most people extend or receive help often in the course of daily living. But the person who automatically aids a friend overloaded with packages or who picks up a passerby's dropped pencil may hesitate to extend similar courtesies to a person who is mobility impaired.

> People have been told that they should not help disabled persons, that we prefer to be independent and do things for ourselves. This notion is not totally false, but it certainly has been overdone. Occasional help from friends and strangers makes my life easier, and I am glad to receive it.

> I think an offer of assistance is appropriate any time another person appears to be having some difficulty. I almost always appreciate an offer of help, whether or not I accept it.

How much help a person chooses to accept is a matter of personal preference. Some mobility-impaired people enjoy assistance any time it makes things go more smoothly or more quickly. Others prefer to receive help only when it is truly necessary.

> I'm slow doing things with my hands, and I'm an impatient person by nature. When I'm taking a long time to do something and someone comes along and helps me do it more quickly, that's a pleasure.

> It's nice when people offer to help with things like folding my wheelchair into the car. But I have my own system, and it's easier to do it myself than to try and explain the process to someone else.

Offering help is never the wrong thing to do. It can always be declined if not wanted.

### How to Lend Aid

A common reason for the reluctance to offer help to a mobility-impaired person is the fear of bungling the job. This fear is not entirely unrealistic; it is definitely possible for a well-meaning helper to do more harm

7

than good. But a positive outcome can be almost assured if a certain procedure is followed. To the uninitiated, these recommendations are offered.

Ask whether help is wanted before beginning to assist. There are many reasons why a mobility-impaired person might choose not to accept an offer of aid.

> When I'm in a public place, I sometimes decline assistance from a passerby and get help from an official or employee instead. For example, when traveling, I like to be helped by airline officials because they are well trained in dealing with disabled customers. I don't have to worry that they'll handle a crutch carelessly, and I don't have to do a lot of explaining.

Even if you feel certain that your assistance would be welcome, do not begin helping without his okay. In particular, do not grab him or his crutch, cane, or wheelchair without warning; doing this can throw him off balance.

Act without asking only when there appears to be an immediate physical danger. Even then, proceed with caution. Almost no situation is so bad that it cannot be made worse by an inexperienced rescuer.

If someone is already helping and it appears that additional assistance may be in order, get instructions from the mobility-impaired person directly, not the helper. The mobility-impaired person is an expert on his needs; the current helper might know less than you do.

Be prepared to take no for an answer. If you are told that help is not wanted, believe it, and take no offense.

> I use a wheelchair sometimes. At a wedding recently, a relative offered to help push me around. I get around quite well by myself, but he was cheerfully insistent. After a couple hours of talking to his friends instead of my own, posing in pictures with him, and doing all the things he wanted to do, I finally had to say, "Thank you, but that's really enough help."

If the offer of help is accepted, find out specifically what needs to be done. The best way of doing something is not always obvious.

> At a car wash, the attendant offered to help me put my wheelchair into the car. The chair is easy to fold if you know how, but she didn't stop to listen to my instructions. She just started pulling parts off the chair, really making mincemeat of it, trying to fit it into the car. It took quite a while for me to put it together again later.

After hearing the instructions, proceed only if you are sure you understand what needs to be done and feel capable of doing it.

Handle the matter as unobtrusively as possible. Many mobility-impaired people feel that their impairment makes them conspicuous, and they prefer that any hoopla surrounding them be kept to a minimum.

Having a physical disability is like being a celebrity or a criminal. You're noticed wherever you go. You can't blend in with the crowd.

Follow through with whatever needs to be done. Like the proverbial cow which gives lots of milk and then kicks over the bucket, the helper who makes a premature exit may negate any prior benefits.

Once when I was getting out of my car, a nice person offered to get my wheelchair out of the trunk. He brought it around and set it next to me, but he took off before I could ask him to put on the brakes. As he jogged away, I watched my wheelchair gather momentum down a hill.

Stay a moment and make sure matters are in hand before taking your leave. Be sure the person is aware that you are departing.

## Doors and Elevators

Closed doors are always awkward for me to cope with, even if someone is pushing my wheelchair. I find people very helpful in other matters, so I'm surprised at how often they just stand by and pretend not to notice as I struggle through doorways.

There are times when almost everyone could use help opening a door, a fact giving rise to the nice custom of lending aid at doorways. Yet the person who normally holds the door with aplomb for a woman carrying a baby might feel unsure of the logistics of performing this act for an approaching mobility-impaired person. Uncertainty leads to inaction, and eyes become transfixed on the designs in the linoleum until the coast is clear—not necessary, if the following rules are observed.

Open the door as the person approaches rather than grabbing it after he has already entered the doorway.

I walk using canes, supporting my weight with my hands. Once I have my hand on a doorknob, that becomes my support for the moment. If someone snatches the door from me while I'm leaning on the knob, I end up on the floor.

Hold the door itself rather than trying to grab an arm, cane, or wheelchair. It is an inexorable law of physics that a single person can get through a doorway more easily than two people attached together.

Having initiated the action, hold the door open long enough for the person to get completely to the other side. Linger a moment longer than seems necessary and check the doorjamb for stray fingers before releasing the door.

Holding an elevator door is much like holding a regular door, except that in this case the door is taking a more active role in the situation. Hold the door open until all parts of the entering person and all related appliances are totally inside, particularly when dealing with elevators of the aggressive, Venus fly-trap variety.

> Sometimes, when a person has helped me into an elevator, he rushes off before I can ask him to press the button for my floor. Since I can't move my hands, I'm then stranded until such time as someone else summons the elevator.

Having helped someone into an elevator, ask whether he can reach the buttons inside. If not, he may be no closer to his destination than if you had continued your study of the linoleum.

### Pushing a Wheelchair

> A passerby stopped to help push me across a landing. We were approaching a ledge and picking up speed, and I kept wondering when she was going to stop or turn. Suddenly, I realized that she had already let go and gone on her way.

Almost all wheelchair users have had negative experiences when being pushed. Many have, consequently, come to regard this type of help with a certain lack of enthusiasm. Nevertheless, there are times when such offers are appropriate and appreciated, if certain procedures are followed.

Never begin pushing a chair without first asking the occupant whether help is desired. An unexpected push will result in two people steering one chair, probably into the china cabinet. More importantly, never release the chair without first making this intention known, especially on a downgrade, upgrade, or when heading toward an interesting topographical feature.

A key factor determining the usefulness of a push is whether or not the chair is motorized. A motorized chair is designed to be propelled on its own and steered by the occupant (via a wand operated by the hand or chin). A helpful push by another party may be greeted with a reaction similar to that of a motorcyclist receiving an extra nudge as he slows to round a curve.

But motorized wheelchairs are somewhat delicate, and they do tend to break down. A person who does not want or need a push when the chair is working usually welcomes this help when it breaks down.

A few additional exceptions to the hands-off rule for motorized chairs: if the motor is not adequate to propel the chair up a steep ramp; if the wheels are not gripping well because of a slick surface, a steep incline, or wet weather; if an especially thick carpet or bumpy street surface is causing trouble; if the situation is unusually tricky, as when maneuvering the chair into a tight corner. But the importance of first asking whether help is wanted cannot be overstressed. A precarious situation is the least welcome time for a surprise shove.

Help is more likely to be appreciated with a manual chair, one that has no motor. With this type of chair, the occupant pushes the wheels with his hands, a process that can get tiring.

> Normally, I use a motorized chair and don't need any help getting around at work. Occasionally, it's broken and I have to use a manual. I really get tired quickly on those long hallways, but the people I know are so used to seeing me get around by myself that they don't even think to offer me a push. They just smile and wave as I pant by.

Some people in manual wheelchairs like to be pushed in damp weather, on heavy carpeting, on steep upgrades, or simply when they are tired. Others prefer never to be pushed at all. Opinions diverge most sharply on the topic of getting pushed across streets. Some people feel more secure being pushed and steered by an able-bodied person; others claim that the specter of getting pushed into potholes and rammed into curbs makes the threat of oncoming traffic pale in comparison.

Most problems with the pushing of a manual wheelchair stem from the helper's unfamiliarity with the shape and behavior of the chair, coupled with an unwarranted nonchalance. Persons accustomed to pushing shopping carts tend not to realize that wheelchairs are less steady, and that hitting even a small bump in the ground can send the occupant face down onto the pavement.

To the novice, this advice is proffered. Begin pushing cautiously if you are not familiar with the particular chair. Take note of the dimensions of the chair, especially the protrusion of the foot plates. If outside, pay attention to the terrain; avoid soft spots and potholes. Watch where you are going!

> I hate being pushed in malls. The person pushing me always underesti-
> mates how far my feet stick out and my foot plates mash people in the

ankles. I spend the whole time getting dirty looks and saying, "I'm sorry, I'm sorry, excuse me, I'm sorry." It's embarrassing.

As for speed, the safest course is to begin slowly. A wheelchair can gather surprising momentum, and the unsuspecting helper may find himself attached to a vehicle whose velocity is somewhat beyond his control.

Somehow when I'm being pushed, I never end up where I was trying to go. After the person has done me the favor of pushing me, it seems unappreciative to complain about my destination.

Oh yes, before starting to push, do remember to ask where the person wants to go.

## Stairs and Steps

I consider myself an exception among mobility-impaired people, because I have strengths that compensate for my disabilities. I rarely need help of any kind, except when getting up and down stairs.

For people whose impairments affect the legs and feet, the most widespread obstacles in modern cities are stairs, steps, and curbs. The number of steps a person can manage depends on his type of impairment.

Certain people in wheelchairs can handle one or more stairs unassisted, as long as the stairs are not too steep. Others need help. The difference lies in the type of chair and the strength and facility of the individual.

I get around in a motorized wheelchair which is fairly heavy. If I'm alone without someone to help me, one step is the same as a hundred.

To help a person in a wheelchair with a step, the following procedure is advised. Going up the step, lean the chair back to raise the front wheels, and push the chair up frontwards. When going down, ask whether the person prefers to go frontwards or backwards. Either way, raise the front wheels and keep them up until the entire chair is down the step. The occupant should always be tilted towards the back against the backrest instead of towards the front where there is no support. This method increases the probability that, when you get the chair up the step, the person will still be in it.

Mobility-impaired people who walk with difficulty may have trouble with one or more steps, particularly if they are steep. Frequently, a strong railing increases the number of steps a person can handle unassisted.

When approaching steps with a person who walks with difficulty, these measures are recommended. Walk at his side and extend an arm to be used for support and balance. If more help is needed, put your arm around his waist as you ascend or descend. The instinctive action of grabbing a mobility-impaired person by his arm is rarely helpful. This offers little support and may throw him off balance.

When he can negotiate stairs unassisted, take the extra precaution of preceding him down the stairs, following him up. Then if he should begin to stumble, you can block his fall.

## Falls

At work sometimes I lose my balance and fall. One of my co-workers usually helps me up, saying, "Falling down on the job again!"

Occasional falls are a fact of life for many people who have mobility impairments. Although certain falls are virtually unavoidable, many are unwittingly caused by other people. Mishaps can be averted if others simply refrain from unexpectedly touching or bumping mobility-impaired individuals.

People rarely realize how bad my balance is. Once I was talking to a seated man, and he pulled me down to say something private. I totally lost my balance and fell over.

At an airport, a policeman saw me starting to get on an escalator with my wheelchair. He was afraid I'd get hurt, so he grabbed my chair to help me. In the process I fell out of the chair, and my bags, which were in my lap, spilled all over. If he'd left me alone, I'd have been fine. I have strong arms and ride escalators all the time.

Once a fall has occurred, the instinctive action of those nearby is to lend a hand in getting up. Some mobility-impaired people appreciate such help; others can rise more easily on their own.

I slipped on a wet floor in a flower shop, and people came running to help me. Several of them grabbed me by the arms and tried to help me up. I normally use my hands to get myself back up when I fall, and with people pulling on my arms, I just couldn't seem to get a footing. I was on the floor a lot longer than I usually am when no one is there to help me up.

Our advice is as follows. When a person has fallen, ask if assistance is wanted. Or, offer your arm, without grabbing, for the fallen person to take if he needs it.

# 3.

## ARCHITECTURAL BARRIERS

People see me get around the building at work and think that I am that mobile all the time. But my place of employment is a new building, designed to be accessible by wheelchair. It has elevators, curb cutouts, and special parking. When I go other places, a lot of times I can't even get through the front door.

Many buildings have "architectural barriers," features which prevent or hinder access by mobility-impaired people. When planning activities in unfamiliar places, mobility-impaired people need to know in advance whether they will encounter any such barriers. They often count on the cooperation of others in supplying this information.

When my friends invite me to meet them at restaurants or other places unfamiliar to me, I always ask if the building is accessible. Sometimes they say, "It has a step or two at the entrance," and I get there and see six steps, too many for me to manage. People just aren't very observant.

Since every mobility impairment is unique, a barrier for one person will not be a barrier for another. The most common three areas of difficulty are parking places, stairs, and rest rooms. People with mobility-impaired friends and associates can simplify outings by learning to observe these three important architectural features.

Mobility-impaired people have special parking requirements because their vehicles are often oversized and because they may need extra space for the maneuvering of a wheelchair. Also, they may find it problematic to have to park a distance from the building.

A lot of multi-level parking garages don't have sufficient clearance for my van. Usually if I can't find a spot on the ground level, I'm out of luck.

I walk with canes and have poor balance. At night I have trouble crossing dimly lit parking lots with bumps and potholes, so it's important for me to be able to park close to my destination.

The presence of specially designated handicapped parking is an excellent omen. Unless the owner is weak in logistics, it indicates that the

14

structure associated with the parking facility is also accessible to mobility-impaired people.

Able-bodied people tend to take steps, stairs, and curbs for granted. Thus when visiting favorite haunts with new mobility-impaired friends, they are frequently greeted by several extra stairs that were definitely not there the day before.

The number of stairs a person can handle depends on his type of impairment. Sometimes even a single step prevents access. Frequently, a strong railing is necessary or helpful.

> On the phone, they told us that there were no steps at the entrance and most of the dining tables were on the ground floor. All this was true, but the rest rooms turned out to be up a flight of stairs.

The inability to reach a rest room can throw a wrench into an otherwise enjoyable outing. People in wheelchairs, unless they can walk for short distances, need a rest room with a door wide enough to pass through and with sufficient space inside to accommodate the chair. Needs vary, but a hand bar by the commode is necessary or helpful to some mobility-impaired people.

Enthusiasts may be tempted to brave the architectural barriers and simply carry their mobility-impaired friends over, around, and through obstacles; this type of help should never be forced on a person. Some people find it unpleasant or scary to be carried, particularly if similar prior experiences concluded on the pavement. Others prefer not to be dependent on someone else's cool-headedness in case of fire or emergency.

But if all concerned are so inclined, such a plan has possibilities.

> There have been many times when I got to places I didn't think I could get to, just from the support and eagerness of friends. But often, people think that something will be easier than it really is.

A word of advice to would-be helpers. Carefully evaluate the task at hand before deciding whether it falls within your abilities. Consider whether you can cope with the consequences if it turns out that your gusto has outstripped your physical prowess. If you pop your football knee carrying your friend up a flight of steps, will you be able to find two people to carry you both back down?

# 4.

## SOCIALIZING

### Recreation

I like my friends to invite me places, even if they think I can't go. Sometimes, they're right, and I can't. But I for sure can't go if they don't ask me.

Able-bodied people often wonder whether to invite a mobility-impaired person to join in an activity which may be beyond his capabilities. In most cases, the answer is yes; invitations to social events are almost always appreciated, whether or not they are accepted.

Mobility-impaired people can participate in a wide range of activities. Even athletic functions are not automatically out of the question. Swimming and other water activities are possible without full use of the arms and legs. Several types of sports can be done from a wheelchair if the person has adequate strength and control in the arms. In fact, special wheelchairs are made for these purposes.

I play tennis and racquetball from my chair, allowing two bounces instead of one. I scuba dive using extra weights.

When a certain activity is not possible, a person who is mobility impaired may enjoy participating in the outing in a way that is less physically demanding, such as watching or scorekeeping.

I love music, and I like to be invited places where I can watch people dance.

On the other hand, most mobility-impaired people do have certain activities which they cannot enjoy and categorically avoid. Many forms of recreation carry some degree of inconvenience or discomfort, and what is worth the effort for some may not be for others. Every person must decide for himself.

My body doesn't perspire well so I don't do things that would require my being out in the sun during the summer. It's too easy to get overheated.

16

Large crowds are a hassle. There is no way for a wheelchair to move through a crowd without bumping people, and to me, it's just not worth the trouble.

I'm extremely sensitive to loud, sudden noises. I avoid events where there will be firecrackers, popping balloons, or other startling sounds.

The variation in physical abilities and personal preferences is so great that it is useless to try to second-guess any given situation. Our recommendation: if you would enjoy having a certain mobility-impaired person along on an outing, extend an invitation and let him decide whether the event would be feasible and pleasurable.

A male friend once told me, "One of the reasons I'm asking you out is that I don't like to dance and you can't." I loved it! I accepted.

## Advance Notice

When inviting a mobility-impaired person for an outing, give some advance notice if possible. Many mobility-impaired people need extra time to arrange for transportation. Others must space their activities to avoid fatigue or soreness. Some people use a service to help them with dressing and grooming, and this must be scheduled; those who handle these tasks themselves often take longer to do them than able-bodied people, and they cannot always be ready for socializing on short notice.

I use a public transportation service designed for disabled people. It takes me almost anywhere I want to go, but I have to make reservations a week in advance.

I'm in a wheelchair, and it's difficult to sit in one position all day. I need to plan times to lie down, not because I am tired but because I'm sore from sitting. If I have been sitting all day at work, it's difficult to go out in the evening on the spur of the moment. I enjoy an outing more if I can plan for it and get out of my chair for a while ahead of time.

But do not automatically assume that he will be unable to attend an event which is occurring spontaneously. Some mobility-impaired people can be ready at the drop of a hat, given sufficient incentive. A few people, those whose impairments fluctuate, actually prefer to do things on the spur of the moment; they avoid planning social events days or weeks in advance since they do not know whether they will be at their best when the designated time arrives.

## Where to Meet

When selecting a public place for socializing with a mobility-impaired friend, investigate the architectural barriers in advance. If possible, scout out the location in person, then report back to your friend so he can judge whether the spot will be accessible to him.

Phoning ahead to a restaurant or place of business can yield some information regarding accessibility, but absolute faith cannot be placed in this type of communication; able-bodied entrepreneurs and employees often do not recognize architectural barriers or realize their importance. The phrase "Of course our establishment is accessible" should be given roughly the same credence as "One size fits all" or "Even a child can assemble it."

> When the restaurant owner said his place was accessible to someone on crutches, he neglected to mention that the only accessible route was through the delivery entrance. Having to bring my date in through the kitchen didn't do much for the ambience of the evening. To make matters worse, the floor was wet and I nearly fell a couple of times.

When in doubt, ask your friend where he would like to meet. He probably has a repertory of restaurants, cinemas, and other public places which he has found accessible and comfortable.

Do not hesitate to invite him to your home, but understand that private homes and apartments are even more likely than public places to have inconvenient architectural features. He may prefer to have you to his house more often than go to yours.

> Almost none of my friends' homes have bathrooms that are accessible to me. So although I enjoy visiting them now and then, there is a limit to how long I can stay there or how many cups of coffee I can drink.

> It takes me a long time to get dressed to go out, get a taxi both ways, and get undressed again afterwards. Our evening together is a couple of hours longer if my friends can come here instead.

## Getting There

A boyfriend once told me that he had hesitated to ask me out on our first date because he didn't know how to get me and my wheelchair from one place to another. He'd seen me out in public places but could never figure out quite how I had gotten there.

Transportation to and from social events may present certain difficulties to mobility-impaired people. But rarely are these insurmountable. With some accommodations, getting around is almost always feasible.

People with some types of impairments ride easily in regular passenger vehicles, perhaps with some minor provisos.

> If there's a choice of cars when we go out, I like two-door models. The doors are usually a little bigger than on four-door models, and I need the extra space when getting in and out.

> If possible I ride in cars with leather or vinyl seats. It's easier for me to slide in and out across a slick surface than a soft fabric.

For wheelchair users, transportation can be more complicated because the vehicle must accommodate the chair as well as the person. Some manual wheelchairs can be folded to fit into passenger vehicles. Depending on the car and type of wheelchair, the chair can go in the trunk, back seat, or onto a special attachment on the outside of the car. Often, a person will have a larger or motorized wheelchair for everyday use and a smaller one for traveling in an automobile.

Some people can get into the car and fold away the wheelchair unassisted; others need help with the process. To the novice helper, this advice is offered. Find out specifically what to do; no single procedure works best for everybody. Do not attempt the task unless, after listening to directions, you are sure you are strong enough for the job. Try to help the person into the car without unduly messing up his hair, wrinkling his clothes, or otherwise sabotaging his appearance. If, in spite of your best efforts, the person's countenance becomes significantly altered in the process, offer to help rectify matters.

A large vehicle, such as a van, has the advantage of accommodating a wheelchair unfolded; with a ramp or lift for getting in and out, the occupant never needs to leave his chair. A properly equipped van can make a car trip quick and easy for a wheelchair user.

> When we needed milk from the convenience store, my wife always used to go rather than asking me because she thought she could do it more quickly. But we discovered that she actually takes longer than I do. It takes me a little more time to get in and out of the van, but she's a slower driver.

Many wheelchair users own vans and use them as their primary mode of transportation.

Mobility-impaired people who drive and own vehicles generally prefer to use their own cars getting to and from social events. In addition to

being conveniently equipped, these vehicles often have decals or identi-
fiers that allow parking in handicapped-designated parking spots.

> When I go out with friends, sometimes they think they're making it
> easier on me by offering to take their car. But I like to take my van
> because it gives me added independence. I feel that it puts me on more
> equal territory with my able-bodied friends.

In contrast, a mobility-impaired person who does not own a vehicle
may appreciate an offer to provide transportation.

> I use a transportation service to go to and from my job. It works out
> fine since I go at the same time every day. It's difficult for me to use this
> service for social events because it has to be reserved several days in
> advance. If I'm planning to go out with friends, it really simplifies
> things for me if they offer to drive.

### Restaurants

Much socializing has traditionally occurred over food, and today,
friends frequently share meals in restaurants. Although a few mobility-
impaired people avoid restaurants for various reasons (such as difficulty
chewing or difficulty projecting the voice in crowded rooms), most list
eating out as a favorite activity. To the person dining out with a mobility-
impaired companion, the following advice is offered.

Select a restaurant with a roomy arrangement of tables and chairs.
Request a table not too distant from the entry if the restaurant is large or
has dining on more than one level.

> Sometimes the tables are so close, and the seating is so tight, that there
> just isn't room for me and my wheelchair. It's uncomfortable, and I can't
> have a good time when people are always trying to squeeze around me.

Offer to assist with the meal. For a person whose impairment affects
the hands or arms, certain foods may be difficult to cut and eat; you can
make the meal more manageable by doing some preprocessing, such as
cutting meat, slicing corn off of the cob, or removing the rind from
fruits. Many people are less free in public than in private about asking
for such assistance and are appreciative if someone expresses a willingness to help.

> I usually ask if I need help with the food, but in some situations I am
> reluctant to do this, so it's great if someone offers. Recently, I was at a
> professional luncheon where I didn't know anyone very well. It was
> hard to pick out someone to ask for help in cutting the meat.

Volunteer your services prior to ordering rather than later. Your dinner companion may opt to forgo the beef stew and order the barbecued ribs if he knows ahead of time that someone is available to help engineer his attack.

As the meal draws to a close, help guard against premature removal of the plates. Almost everyone who eats in restaurants has, at some time, had his plate snatched away before he was quite finished eating. A mobility-impaired person, if he is a slow eater, may be especially liable to be divested of the last part of his meal. If you catch a glimpse of the server creeping up from behind with an arm outstretched, alert your companion.

Thanks to the women's movement, it is no longer automatic that the check in a restaurant is placed before a male. Similar strides remain to be made for mobility-impaired people, so the check is disproportionately likely to appear in front of an able-bodied person. Naturally, a proximity to the check represents no obligation. The matter of the check should be settled by the diners (preferably before the meal) and should not be affected by the assumptions of the server.

# 5.

## PERSONAL SPACE

Wheelchairs, crutches, or other appliances used to enhance physical abilities are very personal items. They should not be borrowed or handled without permission. In particular, they should not be moved from the reach of the owner.

Most people don't realize that a crutch could break if handled carelessly, causing me considerable inconvenience.

Sometimes at parties, people set their drinks on the tray of my wheelchair as if it were a coffee table. I can't move my hands well enough to set them elsewhere. Until the people come back for their glasses (and sometimes they never do), I'm stuck with them.

When sitting in my wheelchair, I've had people push me to the side if I was in their way, instead of asking me to move. They treat my wheelchair as a piece of equipment and forget that there's a person in it.

Some mobility-impaired people are assisted by service dogs which are specially trained to help them with the daily tasks of living. For example, a dog may carry things, help open heavy doors, retrieve dropped items, or push elevator buttons, greatly expanding the owner's freedom and ability to get around.

Service dogs can be identified by their orange collars. Hard as it sometimes is to ignore a pair of big brown eyes and fuzzy ears, others should refrain from touching, feeding, or distracting these important animals.

I have an especially pretty service dog, and people are always wanting to pet her. For example, in a restaurant, they will say, "She's lying down so she isn't working. Now can I pet her?" I say, "She's most definitely working. She is under my command to lie down, not beg for food, not bother the waitress, and stay out of the way. I wouldn't be able to take her along to all the places I go if she were not trained to do those things."

# 6.

## BUSINESS ETIQUETTE

### For Salespeople and Service Providers

I can't get around a large store easily so it's a big help if the salesperson isn't busy and is willing to spend five or ten minutes with me. She can show me things I otherwise wouldn't realize are available. For example, she might know that there's a blouse over on a sale rack that goes with the skirt I'm looking at and offer to run back and see if they have it in my size. Probably all customers would like this service, but for me it's especially helpful.

As a salesperson or service provider, there are several things you can do to better serve your mobility-impaired customers. The most important of these is to familiarize yourself with the surroundings. Learn the locations of elevators, handicapped-designated parking spots, stairs with sturdy railings, and dressing rooms which can be entered by wheelchair. Be able to answer questions regarding architectural barriers over the telephone and to give useful directions within your establishment. Know where wheelchair-accessible rest rooms are located so you will not have to begin asking fellow employees or calling the architect in Bimini when a customer is ardently awaiting the reply.

Keep floors well swept; stray papers and debris can pose a hazard to someone who walks with difficulty. On wet days, provide mats at entrances so floors will not become slippery with tracked-in water. At a service station or similar establishment, do not ask a person in a manual wheelchair to cross an area with grease or mud on the ground; dirt from the floor will get transferred to his hands and sleeves as he pushes the wheels.

When waiting on a person who is mobility impaired, direct your conversation to the customer himself, whether or not he has an able-bodied companion. Be prepared to spend a little extra time if necessary, but do not automatically assume he will need it.

If I need a lot at the grocery store, I don't want an employee to come around with me right away. I like to look things over first by myself, to

23

determine what I want. Then when I have it all figured out, I ask someone to accompany me and get the things I can't reach.

For a customer in a wheelchair, offer to help reach items that are too high, too low, or in an area which is not accessible to him. Ask if he would like you to slide clothes along racks so he can view them. For someone using crutches, help reach things which are inconveniently situated, such as items on very low shelves.

> Around Christmas time, stores usually have a lot of special displays in their aisles, and my wheelchair is too wide to get around them. That's when I need more help than usual because I can't get to the things I want.

> It's obvious that I can't reach high shelves from my wheelchair, but people don't often realize that I can't reach very low shelves either. The wheelchair would topple if I leaned over too far.

For any mobility-impaired person, offer to help carry items to the dressing room or cashier. Do not automatically assume that a person in a wheelchair needs no help in carrying; items that sit cooperatively in the lap when the chair is stationary can be less obliging once the person starts pushing the wheels. Even if carrying is not a particular problem for him, offer to hold merchandise he has selected while he continues to shop.

> I always shop at the same grocery store because the employees there are so thoughtful. I go through the store in my wheelchair, with a small basket on my lap. The employees always keep an eye out, and when they see my basket is full, they are right there to take it and get me another one.

If you are in a position to do so, consider some ways to make your establishment more serviceable for people who have mobility impairments. Arrange aisles so that wheelchairs can pass through. Provide baskets or carts for use within the store. Verify that wheelchair-accessible rest rooms and dressing rooms are well marked, in working order. Also, review parking conditions and be sure that there is handicapped-designated parking convenient to each major entrance, in an area where the customer will not have to interact with a mechanical entry gate to the parking lot. If possible, see to it that this parking area is in view of a security guard or other employee, to deter violators. Consider offering curb service to customers who are not able to easily enter your establishment.

> Salespeople try their best to be helpful, but often there's only so much they can do. If the aisles are blocked so I can't get through, it's almost impossible for the salesperson to be able to listen to what I want, look

around the store, and find just the right thing. Making the stock more available to me is something only the management can do.

## For Cashiers and Tellers

At the customer services area of my favorite store, they have a high counter which I can't see over. It's hard for me to get someone's attention, since they can't see me down in my wheelchair, and then it's hard to transact any kind of business with a tall wall in front of me.

As an employee of a bank, post office, or retail store, you can do several things to better serve a customer who is mobility impaired. We recommend the following measures.

If at all possible, serve a mobility-impaired customer at a desk or low counter while he transacts his business. A person in a wheelchair will appreciate interacting with a visible human being rather than a dis-embodied voice; a mobility-impaired person who does not use a wheel-chair may find it easier to conduct his business sitting down.

If you cannot avoid serving him at a high counter, offer a customer in a wheelchair a clipboard or phone book to use as a writing surface. Be careful in handing him items; be sure he has them before you let go! Bring heavy items around to him, or route them through a will-call or curb service. You might ask if he prefers money in an envelope, to prevent change from scattering, when handing it at arm's length.

The counter at my bank is so high that the teller has to stand on her very tiptoes to hand me my money, and I have to stretch as high as I can to grab it. It's always touch and go.

If his impairment affects his arms, he may ask you to help get out his money, credit card, or checkbook, or to assist him with paperwork.

I carry coupons to the grocery store, and I have to ask the cashier to get them out for me.

I sometimes ask the cashier to write the check because he can do it so much more quickly and clearly than I. I always caution him not to sign it. I will do that myself. People are so used to signing a check after they write it that they often sign their own name.

In a retail store, offer to help him get merchandise onto the counter or conveyer. If there is a choice of packaging, ask how he would like his purchases wrapped. A person on crutches may appreciate a bag with a handle. A person whose impairment affects the arms might want two smaller packages instead of one large one. Someone in a manual wheelchair may prefer a paper sack to a slippery plastic bag, the former having a better chance of staying in his lap as he pushes the wheels.

If you have the authority, investigate the possibility of making your building easier to enter for people who are mobility impaired. Common obstacles in banks, post offices, and many other buildings are doors which are too heavy for a mobility-impaired person to open unassisted. Also unpopular are automatic doors which close too quickly after the person has (almost) passed through.

> Occasionally at the post office, an employee will try to move me to the front of the line. It's a thoughtful gesture, but I really don't want that kind of special treatment.

### For Restaurant Employees

For restaurant employees who wish to better serve their mobility-impaired customers, we offer these recommendations. First, put a little extra thought into selecting a table.

Seat a mobility-impaired customer at one of your roomier tables. Do not wedge him into a spot where others will be trying to wriggle past his wheelchair or knocking down his crutches. Try to seat a wheelchair user at a table that he can put his legs under; a wheelchair sits higher off the ground than a standard chair and does not fit under all dining tables. Tables with flip ends often work well. Tables that are low or have wide rims do not. Seat a person who uses crutches, a cane, or walker near a wall so he can more easily keep the appliances out of the way. Select a sturdy chair with arms for a person who may have trouble sitting and rising; then, hold the chair steady as he seats himself. In a large or multi-level restaurant, seat any mobility-impaired person reasonably near the entrance. If no nearby table is immediately available, consult with the customer; he may prefer to wait a while rather than having to machete his way to a far corner of a crowded establishment.

> The other day, I went to one of my favorite restaurants. I hadn't been there in a few weeks, and they had added about ten tables. They seated me way in the back, and the tables were so close together that several patrons who were eating their lunch had to get up while I went through with my wheelchair. Naturally, the scene was played in reverse when it was time to leave.

A person who uses a wheelchair may or may not move to a standard chair to eat, depending on his type of impairment, the style of the restaurant's chairs, and his personal preference. If he plans to remain in his wheelchair, walk ahead and remove the standard chair from his spot before he gets there; unless there is plenty of space, the process will require more careful choreography once he arrives. If he prefers to move to a standard chair, help him push himself up to the table after he has made the switch. Do not automatically whisk away his wheelchair; ask for permission before you handle it, and let him know where it will be.

Speak directly to a mobility-impaired customer. Never route your conversation through an able-bodied companion.

If his impairment affects the arms, place bread, salt shakers, appetizer trays, and other items in easy reach for him. Offer to have meats cut up in the kitchen prior to serving and to bring a straw for liquids. If he is dining alone, offer to help him with the salad bar or buffet. Check on him now and then to see if he needs anything; he may not be able to wave you down.

> The people I'm with are usually happy to cut my food, but that means theirs will get cold so I hate to ask them. It's so much nicer if the restaurant employees will do it.

As always, place the check in the center of the table at the close of the meal if there is more than one diner. Do not assume an able-bodied person will be paying for the meal.

If you are in a position to do so, investigate the possibility of making your establishment more accessible to people who have mobility impairments.

> Since I'm not too steady on my feet, it's a big plus if a restaurant has good illumination at the entrance.

> Probably the biggest factor for me is whether or not the place has a rest room that can be entered by wheelchair.

> I was supposed to meet some people at a restaurant, and I drove up and saw that there were four steps. I thought I was going to have to leave, but the parking attendant, seeing the "handicapped" decal on my car, immediately pulled out a wooden ramp which they'd built to fit right over the steps. I was delighted to be able to enter the restaurant with ease.

### For Health Care Professionals

> I go to a wonderful doctor who realizes that I have special requirements and is willing to learn about them. She always says, "If there is anything you need, anything that I'm not doing, feel free to let me know."

Most people find it unnerving to receive even routine medical and dental care. Happily, the individuals drawn to the health professions usually have the concern and sensitivity to make every attempt to minimize the stress. For health care professionals striving to provide optimum care to mobility-impaired patients, we offer these recommendations.

When speaking to a mobility-impaired patient on the phone, be able to accurately report the architectural barriers he can expect to encounter upon his arrival. Tell him the locations of handicapped-designated parking areas, ramps, and elevators, to save him from having to discover a workable route to your office through a series of exploratory probes. Discuss whether or not he will need help entering the building; flagging down a passerby for assistance is not always so easy.

In your waiting room, have at least one sturdy, medium-height chair with arms, for a person who has difficulty sitting down and rising. Arrange the area with some leeway; do not fill it with so many chairs and tables that a person in a wheelchair will have to be sardined into a walkway as he waits for his appointment.

If you are expecting a mobility-impaired patient, be sure there is a way for him to get your attention when he arrives. Place your bell or buzzer where it can be reached from a wheelchair, and do not put a big potted plant in front of it! A patient whose impairment affects the arms may not be able to ring any type of bell; keep an eye on the reception area when his appointment time is near so he will not have to cool his heels for too long.

Allot ample time for his visit, and be sure that staff is available to provide the extra services that he may require. For example, a person in a wheelchair may ask for some help maneuvering through narrow halls, using the rest room, or transferring from the wheelchair to the examining table. A person with an impairment affecting the arms may request help with paperwork.

> They often don't realize that it takes some extra time for me to get dressed and undressed. It's nice when a nurse offers to help me, but it still can't get done quite as fast as they seem to expect.

> I have a dentist who always bends over backwards to accommodate me. Whenever she's expecting me, she makes sure to have someone there to help lift me out of my wheelchair into the dental chair because she's not strong enough to do it alone.

Tell other members of the staff if the patient has particular needs. Be sure that others know about any kind of special arrangements you may have made with him; do not force him to do his own explaining to person after person.

When I'm in the hospital, meals are never served in a way that I can eat them. The meat isn't cut up, the milk carton isn't opened, and so on, and I don't have the manual dexterity to do these things myself. Unless I want to just stare at my meal, I have to be aggressive and not let the person delivering the meal leave without helping me out. Each day it's a different person who brings the food, and some are more receptive to my requests than others.

Once in a hospital, I was preparing to shower, and the nurse told me to push the emergency button when I was finished so he could help me get out. He forgot to tell the other people on the floor that I was going to do this, and when I pressed the button, a half dozen people came running to my room in a frenzy. It was embarrassing.

Refrain from moving him around unnecessarily during the course of his visit. Sometimes it is easier to bring instruments or paperwork to the patient than to ask him to move to another room. Consider whether a person who uses a wheelchair can be treated or examined in his chair, without the compromise of his care.

I used to put off going to the eye doctor, in part because it was so much trouble getting out of my wheelchair and up onto that high examining chair. I needed two people to help me transfer each way, and it was a real production. Now I found a terrific eye doctor who has move-able instruments and who will examine me in my wheelchair. It's a breeze.

Never move his wheelchair, walker, or other appliance out of his reach without permission. If you have his okay to move it, let him know where it will be.

Realize that he may have unique needs, and allow him to voice them. Instruct your staff that he may participate in directing his own care to a greater degree than other patients.

In the hospital, nurses are used to doing what the doctor has written on the chart, and they tend not to take seriously any additional instructions from the patient. I need to be turned in my bed frequently, and I have a hard time getting anyone to do this.

Respect the fact that he may have prearranged his transportation and may not be able to alter his plans on short notice. Make every effort to see him on schedule and to have him ready at the expected time.

If you are in a position to do so, investigate the possibility of making your building more accessible to people who are mobility impaired. In large hospitals, a common complaint is that handicapped-designated parking is not convenient to each of the many entrances. In private offices, accessible rest rooms are often lacking; in addition, doors between rooms are sometimes too narrow to allow wheelchairs to pass. In all sorts of medical facilities, even those constructed specifically to be accessible, a common complaint is the lack of space to maneuver.

> Most semi-private rooms in hospitals are so cramped I can't move around. There are the two beds, the little tables that come across the beds, chairs for visitors, the curtain area. There is another person in the next bed who probably doesn't want to be bothered by me trying to shimmy my way around all the obstacles. So even though the rest room itself is built to be wheelchair accessible, I can't get to it without calling the nurse.

# 7.

## CONVERSATION

### Talking with a Wheelchair User

When I'm talking to someone who's standing, there's only so long I can look up at her or him. After a while, I have to give up and look straight ahead. People think they're boring me, when really I just have a kink in my neck.

When having a conversation with a person in a wheelchair, make an effort to position yourself so that it will not be uncomfortable for him to look at you. Usually it is best for you to seat yourself, so as to be at eye level with him, but sometimes a chair is not readily available and lugging one over would be disproportionately troublesome. For a short conversation, do whatever seems easiest.

If you choose to remain standing, do not edge in so close as to force your listener into a dental-exam position. The taller you are, the more distance you should allow.

Outdoors on a bright day, be on the alert for the pained grimace that indicates your head is creating a partial eclipse of the sun. Pull up a lawn chair, face the sun yourself, or move the conversation to a shadier spot.

Find a seat if the conversation will be extended. If no chairs or sitting surfaces are available, suggest moving the conversation elsewhere. Do not crouch, squat, or assume any position typified by the loud creaking of joints or visible straining of seams. Such postures rapidly become painful, and, except in the most informal of settings, they are unduly conspicuous.

Whether standing or sitting, situate yourself face to face with the other person, rather than to his side.

It's hard for me to turn my body in my wheelchair. People have a tendency to stand off at an angle while talking to me, and it's a strain trying to look at them. Sometimes I'll roll my wheelchair around to be facing them, but if I don't say something about it, they often simply reposition themselves to my side. We end up moving in backward circles for the duration of the conversation.

31

### Topics of Conversation

I don't think anything is ever accomplished by a person not saying what's on his mind.

An impairment is often a source of curiosity. People wonder how it occurred and how it affects daily life. Most mobility-impaired people have been asked about these things so much as to be tempted to distribute photocopies. Still, many continue to welcome questions.

It's important to tell people a little about my impairment. Otherwise, they wonder. It's great if people can ask questions. Sometimes they are afraid they'll hurt my feelings. They won't.

Occasionally, people ask my wife about my disability when I'm not around. I prefer that they ask me directly. I like knowing that they're interested.

Having a physical impairment carries its share of frustrations, and others may feel empathy with the person facing these. Few mobility-impaired people object to the expression of empathy, provided the speaker is sincere.

I don't like it when a total stranger says, "I know exactly how you feel," since this is obviously untrue. But I do feel good when a friend or acquaintance tries to understand the problems I have.

Humor can be found in all human conditions; disability is no exception. Situations arise where lighthearted thoughts come to mind, and there is rarely a reason not to express them.

Both my husband and I use wheelchairs. When I first told my family about our engagement, my granddaughter said, "I can hardly wait to see you rolling down the aisle!"

I work in electrical engineering. My coworkers always joke about wanting to put a remote control on my motorized wheelchair so they'd be able to just push a button whenever they needed to talk to me.

My best friend and I are both disabled. He's a double amputee, so when we get into an argument, I say, "You don't have a leg to stand on!"

Humor is one of the delights of life. It can be enjoyed by all when it is offered in the spirit of sharing and good will.

### Private Topics

In the early days of the space program, there was less general curiosity about how the force of gravity had been defied than about what the astronaut did, stuck up there in that little capsule, when nature called. Similar curiosities exist about people with certain types of mobility impairments. Like astronauts, some mobility-impaired people do not mind explaining the matter, and others do. For the inquisitive, our advice is as follows.

If the topic is initially broached by the mobility-impaired person, feel free to ask further questions. Otherwise, be guided by the nature of your relationship. If you consider yourself a casual friend or passing acquaintance, refrain from intruding on his privacy.

> A friend asked me if I used a catheter. It was a very close friend, and there was no one else around, so I had no problem with that question.
> It depends on who is asking. You have to be awfully close.

Among topics for speculation, sexual functioning follows hot on the heels of bodily elimination. Again, bring up this subject only with a close friend, in the spirit of sharing rather than interrogation.

If your questions stem from more than idle curiosity, by all means ask them. Mobility impairments do not affect sexual feelings; they merely affect the manner in which these feelings are expressed.

# 8.

## ENTERTAINING

### Arrival

When I'm invited to somebody's house, I like to know ahead of time what barriers I'm going to encounter. If there are any steps, or if the bathroom is on the second floor, I would appreciate knowing that. I hate to be surprised.

When a mobility-impaired person is invited to the home of a friend, he has to evaluate the architectural barriers of the building before deciding whether to accept. As a prospective host, you can help by providing a brief description of your home when you extend the invitation. The key pieces of information will be the availability of parking, the presence of stairs, and the location and accessibility of the rest room.

Certain barriers can be overcome if you or another person will be able and willing to give the necessary assistance. However, a mobility-impaired person may have limits to the type of help he is comfortable receiving. For example, some people find it acceptable to receive help, using an inaccessible rest room; others do not. Some find it acceptable to be carried up stairs in order to enter the home; others prefer to stick with the more conventional modes of locomotion.

I've had people carry me up three flights of steps. As long as they are willing to do it, it doesn't bother me. Some people are afraid to pick me up, they think I'll break in half. I tell them, "Don't worry, I've been dropped more times than I can remember."

The consequences of a fall and broken bones would put me down for a very long time. So I avoid being carried and try to be careful about getting into dangerous situations.

Whatever the case, it is preferable to discuss these issues in advance rather than to try to deal with them on the fly. If the situation is mutually agreeable and the invitation is accepted, the following measures will help make the visit a success.

Arrange some signal to announce the arrival of a guest who will need assistance entering the home. For example, he might honk a horn when he reaches the front porch. In the event that you have neglected to make such arrangements, the roast is drying out, and you wonder why your company has not arrived, look out the front window.

Help a guest in a wheelchair situate himself where he can easily face everyone else. Select a spot where the wheelchair does not block the movement of others, so that he will not be bothered by people squeezing by and stepping over him during the visit.

For a person who has difficulty sitting down and rising, find a sturdy chair which is not on rollers and which has a back and arms. Avoid low, soft chairs and mushy couches; these can permanently entrap anyone who is not athletically inclined. Hold the chair steady as he sits, and extend an arm, without grabbing, for him to take when he rises.

Seat a guest who uses canes or crutches near a wall on which to lean the appliances. They should never be out of reach.

Keep dogs and other large pets in another room, and bring them out only under close supervision. This admonition is not limited to animals who routinely terrorize the mailman; even dogs who are normally cavalier around strangers may revert to primitive behavior at the approach of an unusual moving object such as a crutch, walker, or wheelchair.

Set the thermostat at a moderate level. With certain types of impairments, the body may lose some of its ability to warm or cool itself. If the temperature is unusually high or low, your guest could become uncomfortable.

> I appreciate hosts taking special consideration of my handicap. But I don't like them to make too big a fuss. I can't relax if they don't relax.

## Planning Menus

> My digestive system just can't take certain foods, so I appreciate it when a hostess lets me know what's going to be served. Then I don't have to worry and wonder about it. It's embarrassing for me to get to a party and have to ask that my food be served differently from everyone else's.

A mobility impairment may have an impact on the types of foods a person can eat and enjoy. When inviting a mobility-impaired person for a meal, you can avoid problems by keeping certain facts in mind.

A mobility impairment is sometimes accompanied by digestive difficulties. Rich or spicy foods typically wreak the most havoc; take pause before deciding to fix your special Thermonuclear Chili con Carne.

For a person with an impairment of the arms or hands, certain foods might be awkward to eat. Common culprits are stuffed finger foods, such as tacos, which tend to fall apart. Also problematic are foods which must be chased around the plate, such as peas, or foods which are difficult to cut, such as poultry with bones, or foods which have a life of their own, such as spaghetti.

> I sometimes have trouble with big fat sandwiches, especially on hard rolls. I can't grab onto them well, and the meat tends to gradually slide out the back. I end up getting just the bread.

Often a very minor change in the menu can make the meal easier to eat. For example, melon chunks are less troublesome than wedges with rind. As a rule, anything that can be eaten with one hand is more manageable than something that requires the coordination of two hands.

> Certain foods are messy for me to eat. If I go to the home of someone I don't know very well, I don't like to be served these foods. But if I'm visiting friends who don't mind giving me a hand, then any dish is fine.

### Serving Meals

In addition to giving some forethought to the menu, a host can do the following things to make a meal more enjoyable for a mobility-impaired guest.

For a wheelchair user, try to serve on a table that is large and fairly high.

> If a table is less than 30 inches off the floor, or if there's a pedestal in the middle, I can't get my wheelchair under it. I end up sitting an arm's length from the table while I eat, and that's a long way not to drip the sauce.

Ask about seating preferences. A person who has difficulty turning his body may enjoy sitting at the head of the table, where he can easily see the other people. A person in a wheelchair might prefer a middle seat, where the legs of the table are not in the way. A person who uses a cane or crutches will be most comfortable near a wall on which to lean the appliance.

Do not pile food high on a small plate. Do not fill a glass so full that he has to wait for some to evaporate before he dares to lift it.

Ask whether certain utensils would make the meal more manageable. For example, a cup might be easier to handle than a glass, which may get slippery. A bowl in place of a salad plate can deter the getaway of cherry tomatoes. A straw might be helpful with liquids or soups.

For a guest with an impairment affecting the hands, offer to help cut meat from bones, peel rind from fruit, or otherwise tame foods into submission. But keep such offers low-keyed and do not belabor the issue.

> It's nice if the host says a single time, "Let me know if there is anything I can do for you," rather than repeatedly interrupting the whole conversation and asking in front of everyone whether I need another napkin, want my meat cut, etc.

If the degree of impairment or rebelliousness of the food warrants it, offer to feed your guest all or part of the meal.

> I like some help towards the end of the meal. By then my arms get tired, and I can't get the last few lima beans or grains of rice onto my fork and into my mouth.

When helping a person with more than a few mouthfuls, alternate feeding him and eating your own meal.

> When a certain friend feeds me at social gatherings, often she will give me my entire meal before she starts to eat. This always makes me feel like I should be eating as fast as I can so that her food doesn't get too cold. I would prefer to have her take a bite, then me, then her, so that we're eating together.

Occasionally ask your guest which food he would like next. This saves him an eternity of eyeing the Veal Oscar while being administered successive mouthfuls of boiled Brussels sprouts.

A guest with an impairment of the hands or arms may take longer to eat than the others present. Help pace the meal by serving it in courses, with a short wait after each course, so the others do not get too far ahead of him.

## Parties

> If I don't know anybody at a party, I feel somewhat isolated. People usually stand around in circles. Since I'm always sitting, it's difficult for me to just introduce myself.

At a party where a large number of people are standing, a person in a wheelchair or a person who must sit may find it difficult to mix. From a belt-level vantage point, one cannot easily make eye contact and start a conversation. In addition, a mobility-impaired person may lack a strong voice projection, and if the room is noisy, the lone voice from below may be lost in the general din.

A major role of a host at a party is to introduce people and start conversations. To a mobility-impaired guest, introductions can make the difference between a dull evening and an enjoyable get-together.

In addition to helping people mix, a host can take a few other measures to make the event proceed more smoothly. To the prospective party-giver, these recommendations are offered.

Prepare for the party by assessing the room for clutter. People in wheelchairs will feel more comfortable at a gathering where there is enough space to mill around without scraping ankles and bumping piano legs. Sometimes just a slight rearrangement of furniture with the removal of some small pieces can make the room significantly more navigable. Remove small throw rugs, which can become tangled in wheels or slide around under a cane.

Provide ample seating. The presence of chairs and couches will encourage others to sit, so that the seated mobility-impaired person will feel less subterranean.

When the guests arrive, help situate a mobility-impaired person in a spot where he can stay for a while. For a wheelchair user, find a place where he can socialize without blocking the flow of foot traffic, so that people will not be constantly jostling past him.

> When I go to a large party, I like to be able to seat myself so my back isn't to someone. It's nice to be able to be in the group but not at the center of the group. It's awkward to try to turn around and converse with someone behind me.

For a guest who has difficulty walking and will be sitting for most of the party, find a sturdy and comfortable chair which is not too removed from the center of activity.

Point out the location of the rest room. Some mobility-impaired people have requirements that preclude lengthy hunting expeditions when the time comes to use the facilities. Others like a chance to assess the rest room for accessibility in advance.

> If I'm embarking on an evening of food and drink, I like to know ahead of time how easy it will be to get in and out of the rest room. A lot of times, if I see that the powder room is small, I ask if I can use the master bathroom, which is usually larger.

Serve snacks and drinks on a low table rather than a high counter, which would be inaccessible to wheelchair users. Offer to bring some refreshments to a mobility-impaired guest now and then.

Well intentioned able-bodied guests may become overzealous in catering to a person with a reduced ability to get around. If food seems to be accumulating around a mobility-impaired person at an alarming rate, offer to discretely siphon some off.

At a party recently, every new person I met brought me some more refreshments. It was hard to refuse plates of snacks that had already been prepared for me, and the food was coming faster than I could eat it. It was definitely too much of a good thing.

# 9.

## VISITING

Entertaining friends at home is a favorite activity of a great number of mobility-impaired people. Many entertain more often than visit because transportation is a problem or because their friends' homes are not accessible to them. To the prospective guest, the following recommendations are offered.

Volunteer to help with carrying or whatever else might be difficult for your host to do.

> All the things I use most are kept low where I can reach them. But when people come over and I don't want to use the everyday dishes, I ask them to get down the good china.

> Since my balance is precarious, I usually ask my guests for some help in serving. If there's a big tray of appetizers to be carried, I figure my guests would rather eat them than wear them so I just ask someone else to carry it.

Take some initiative in seeing to your own needs. When a refreshment is offered, express your willingness to serve yourself, but if the host indicates he would rather serve you, do not protest or hurdle-race him to the kitchen. And if you are told, "Help yourself to anything you want," do not interpret this statement too literally.

> It's hard for me to get up and sit down. So in a casual situation, I usually invite my guests to help themselves to more coffee or whatever. However on those rare occasions when I'm entertaining more formally, I feel better if my husband or I serve our guests.

Keep your possessions off the floor if the host or other guests use a wheelchair or walk with difficulty. Do not drop a purse or sweater where it will be in the way.

At the end of the visit, do not leave things where your host will have difficulty retrieving them. For example, if you have moved a heavy chair from its normal position, return it to its usual spot before you go. If your host is in a wheelchair, do not leave empty glasses up on a high mantel for him to try to spirit back down after you have gone.

Ask whether there is anything you can do before you leave. But refrain from doing more than is requested. If you are gripped with the urge to rearrange the pantry, exercise some restraint.

I can't reach the kitchen cabinets from my wheelchair so I leave the dishes in the dish rack after I wash them. It never fails, if I leave someone unsupervised in the vicinity of my kitchen, he puts away my dishes. Then when I discover that they are gone, I have to call another person to come over and put them back in the rack.

# 10.

## CHILDREN

I was in a restaurant with a man who had lost a leg and used crutches. Two children and a mother passed in front of us, and the kids stared at us and started asking questions. The mother pulled them along, whispering, "Don't stare!" My dinner companion turned to me and said, "You know, because of people like us, a lot of kids have one arm longer than the other."

People who have mobility impairments frequently arouse the curiosity of children. Parents yearn for instant invisibility as their offspring zero in on the unfamiliar, point fingers, and begin making loud, blunt queries.

Once a child has made an inquiry within earshot of the person in question, it rarely palliates the matter to knock her on the head and yank her away. Nor does it improve the situation to try to distract her with a nearby bicycle display. This does nothing to save the moment, does not enlighten the child, and can get expensive.

Many mobility-impaired people prefer that the questions of children be referred directly to them. Others prefer that the parent provide the answers.

In a store, a child looked at me and asked resoundingly, "Daddy, why does that lady have such fat feet?" If the father could have buried himself, he would have. I said, "My feet are fat because they stay in one position all day." The child was satisfied, and the father seemed extremely relieved.

I dislike an adult telling a child not to ask me questions. I feel strongly that when a child asks an honest question, he deserves an honest answer.

I haven't been around kids much and don't generally have a rapport with them. When a child is staring and asking questions about me, I would prefer that the parent do the explaining, without involving me.

Our recommendation to parents is as follows. Do not rebuke your child for expressing her natural curiosity. If the mobility-impaired person shows a willingness to participate in the conversation, direct your child's questions to him. Otherwise, answer the questions yourself, to the best of your ability. Absolutely, intercede if your child's curiosity leads to physical mischief. Allowing a child to handle a wheelchair or other appliance without permission of the owner is tempting fate.

A child in a department store came and grabbed the controls of my motorized wheelchair. He had seen me operating it and thought he could, too. We wiped out two dress racks before I could regain command of the situation.

Virtually all mobility-impaired people agree emphatically that a child's questions about disability, its cause, its appearance, or its related appliances, should not be brushed aside.

I feel a child's initial curiosity must be satisfied. The child should be given direct and complete answers to his questions. The way the parent deals with the situation can make a big difference in how the child grows up accepting disabilities of any kind.

## Section Two

## ETIQUETTE WITH VISUALLY IMPAIRED PEOPLE

# 11.

## SOME PRELIMINARIES

The media portray blind people in two categories: those who are totally helpless and can't do anything, and those who are superhuman and can do everything. There's never the normal everyday guy like me who manages to do most things but needs a little help now and then.

This section deals with blindness and other impairments of vision which are not satisfactorily corrected with eyeglasses or medical remedies. Visual impairments take a wide variety of forms, and a single impairment can fluctuate from day to day. The recommendations offered in this section are designed to be general, to apply to the many, diverse types of diminished or distorted vision. The reader does not need to understand the exact nature of a particular impairment in order to implement these suggestions. He simply needs to know that an impairment exists.

Because I can see some things very well, people have trouble believing that I really am visually impaired. When I focus on something, only a very small part of it looks clear to me. The rest is hazy. I have a hard time getting an overall picture of what things look like.

Unless it is specifically pointed out, a visual impairment is not always obvious to the casual observer. Some visually impaired people wear eyeglasses which improve their vision to some degree. Others wear non-prescription tinted lenses to ease light sensitivity. Certain visually impaired people use either a guide dog or a long cane to help them get around. A guide dog is an animal which has been specially trained to lead the way safely as its owner walks. It wears a harness with a short strap rather than the long leash which an ordinary pet would wear. A cane is used to scan the ground ahead and feel for obstacles. Most often, it is light colored, with or without a red or yellow tip.

Many people appear to have better vision than they really do. An increased attention to the other senses, combined with a good memory, can partially compensate for the lack of clear sight.

47

When I travel on business trips without my wife, I put a lot of effort into memorizing the way to my hotel room. I count the number of doors from the elevator, so I won't have to strain to see room numbers each time I go. It would be embarrassing if I had my nose up to a door and a strange woman opened it.

People who are visually impaired must contend not only with a physical limitation but also with widespread misconceptions about their impairment; some are hard pressed to say which of the two causes more problems. It is the purpose of this section to help sighted people rid themselves of false assumptions and learn to feel at ease with visually impaired people.

# 12.

## PRACTICALITIES

### When to Lend Aid

I admire people who stop to help. I know that it's so much easier to steer clear.

Most people enjoy extending help to others when the occasion arises. But even the most well intentioned individuals sometimes hesitate to lend aid to someone who is visually impaired. This reserve stems in part from an inability to determine whether help is needed in a given circumstance. A person unfamiliar with visual impairments may not be able to distinguish a situation that is on shaky ground from one that is progressing according to standard operating procedure.

> Sometimes I like to explore a place on my own. We have a new grocery store at the corner, and I want to learn where everything is. While I'm investigating, I look as though I'm lost as a goose, and people keep trying to help me. But I'm just doing what I need to do to get myself oriented.

Rather than chance misreading a situation and volunteering inappropriately, some would-be helpers prefer to wait until assistance is specifically requested. This is a valid course of action. However, a visually impaired person may want help and not know anyone is nearby. Or, she may hear many people and have trouble deciding whom to approach. If she cannot see well enough to make out facial expressions and body language, she may be reluctant to risk flagging down someone who is in a hurry or otherwise disinclined to stop and help. An explicit offer of assistance can spare her much uncertainty and conjecture.

Our recommendation is as follows. If you see a need and are willing to help, step forward. But take no offense if your offer is politely declined.

> It is reassuring to know that I am not alone and that help is available if I need it. But I want the freedom to say no. Some people get offended when I refuse their help, and I worry that they'll never offer to help a blind person again.

It's a delicate balance. I want and need help sometimes, but I also want to be independent. It makes me feel good to do certain things by myself, even if someone else might be able to do them more quickly or easily. So at times I say, "No, thanks," to an offer of help.

Occasionally, an offer of assistance may be met with a snarl. If you do happen to extend an offer to someone who woke up on the wrong side of the bed that morning, do not be discouraged from volunteering with the next person. Offering help is never the wrong thing to do.

## How to Lend Aid

The single most useful thing a friend or stranger can do for a visually impaired person is to furnish relevant information about the immediate surroundings. Often just a few words can make a welcome difference.

In a bank, sometimes a nice person will point me to the window with the shortest line.

In public rest rooms, the location of the towel dispenser or hand drier varies a lot. If I reach over where I think it should be and it's there, good. If it's not there, a tip from someone else can spare me a lot of hunting.

If I'm waiting for a bus, it helps if someone tells me the route numbers of the different buses that come by. That saves me from having to go up into each bus and ask the driver. Inside, it's marvelous if someone will' say, "There's an empty seat four rows back." Then I don't have to touch every seat looking for a place to sit.

If I drop something outside, it's so helpful if someone picks it up for me or tells me where it is. Otherwise, I might have to just leave it. I wouldn't spend a very long time trying to find something unless it was valuable.

I want to know about any kind of obstacles that aren't usually there. If there's a scaffold in a hallway or a hole in a street near me, I would like to be told about it so I can avoid it.

Help to a visually impaired person is most likely to be appreciated if the following ground rules are observed. Furnish simple information without hesitation, any time it seems appropriate; if you see a "wet paint" sign strategic to a visually impaired person, do not waste time debating whether to point it out. But for any active form of assistance, always ask first whether help is wanted. If your offer is accepted, be sure you understand what needs to be done before initiating any action.

People tend to make assumptions without stopping to listen to me. It's happened more than once that I was standing on a street corner and a stranger pulled me across a street I was not planning to cross.

Avoid drawing undue attention to yourself and the person you are helping. For example, if you are providing information, do not speak at a volume that would cause heads to turn.

Once you have begun lending aid, follow it through to the natural conclusion. For instance, if you are helping someone cross a street, be sure to see her safely up the opposite curb. If you are showing her your favorite shortcut through back alleys, do not leave her to find her own way through the final twist of the maze.

A few times, someone has helped me hail a cab and then disappeared before I got in or even knew the cab was there. It's a tremendous help if the person waits a minute, to be sure I'm getting into the right car!

### Giving Directions

I can't make heads or tails of the things some people say to me when they give me directions. One man told me, "Go straight up and to the left." I thought to myself, "If I had a beanie with a propeller on top, I could do that."

When giving directions to a visually impaired person, the first step is the most important: decide whether you really know where the desired location is! If you are hazy about your facts, let her ask someone else; do not just cross your fingers and take a stab at it.

If you decide you are qualified to help, be as specific as possible with your information. Whenever you can, describe distances using numbers. For example, you might say, "It's four blocks straight ahead."

Inside a building, it's helpful if people tell me how many doors I'll pass. Then I can use my cane to trail along the wall and count the doors.

It's a lot easier if people say, "Go three blocks," rather than, "Go to Madison Street." There are rarely street signs on all four corners of an intersection, and I can't read a street sign unless I get right up to it.

When describing turns or curves, use well-defined terms such as "left," "right," "north," or "clockwise" rather than vague terms such as "over there" or "veer off." If you are facing the person, do not confuse your left with her left. When giving directions by the compass (north, south, east, west), first tell her which way she is facing.

People will say, "It's across the street from such and such," when it's not really directly across the street. They forget that I take them literally.

Describe anything out of the ordinary along the way, especially things that could pose safety hazards. For example, if there is construction along the sidewalk, or if a street has one-way traffic, mention that.

If the person has some vision, tell her about a few landmarks that she will pass. Having some prominent features to watch for will help keep her oriented, especially in parking lots or other broad expanses of unstructured space. Fire hydrants are good landmarks to mention, since they are usually brightly colored. Large trees or distinctive buildings are also good choices.

Be as complete as possible, but do not give a lot of extraneous explanation. Most people can only absorb a certain amount of information at a time; beyond that, additional facts only muddle the picture.

Some places are simply hard to find. If you suspect that, after hearing your very best set of directions, the person would end up circling the city dump, you might offer to act as escort.

> People sometimes offer to just walk with me to the place I'm looking for. If I'm not totally lost and frustrated, I'd rather try to follow their directions. But if I have been given three or four sets of directions and have blown every one of them, then I'm glad when someone offers to take me.

## Walking

When traveling on foot, visually impaired people need to keep mental track of where they are, use their other senses to maintain their course, and continually stay alert to anything out of the ordinary. Even old hands occasionally find the process tiring and welcome the respite of walking with a sighted companion.

> When a friend is going in my direction, I say, "Hey, can I grab on? Then I won't have to concentrate." Sighted people can walk along and glance around and know where they are. But when I walk, I have to be on my toes all the time. Otherwise I might start walking crooked or forget where I am in relation to where I'm going. If I have a choice, I will always go with a sighted friend.

When you walk with a person who is visually impaired, offer her your arm. She may be able to walk more quickly and confidently while holding onto you. If you are of roughly equal height, she will probably take your arm at or above the elbow. Do not try to reverse the situation and clutch her arm; it is impossible to proceed in a coordinated fashion while in this position.

> It's much easier if I take your arm than if you take mine. If you take my arm, you will have to steer me this way and that way, whereas if I take yours, I can easily follow you. I've had people practically carry me across the street, when all they had to do was offer me their arm and walk in their normal manner.

If she prefers not to hold your arm, walk closely enough for her to reach over and touch you. Try not to get separated in crowds. And respect the fact that, even with your presence, she is probably expending more mental effort than a sighted person would.

> Sometimes I'm walking along with friends, and they're trying to have this big profound conversation with me. I tell them, "Talk to me later." It boggles my mind to try to talk to them and also pay attention to where I'm going.

When a visually impaired person takes your arm, walk slightly ahead and proceed normally. Avoid sudden turns or jerky movements.

> You can really tell a great deal about the terrain when you walk with someone and touch him. You can tell when he steps up or down or sidesteps an obstruction.

> Whether or not I take someone's arm, I need to walk slightly behind and follow the other person's lead. The problem is, I'm a senior, and young people tend to want to let me go first out of courtesy.

Walk at your usual speed unless the ground is rough or there are an unusual number of obstacles. It is easier for another person to follow your body movements if you walk at a steady pace and do not continually stop or slow down without cause.

When approaching a step, stairway, elevator, or anything out of the ordinary, pause and briefly describe what is ahead. Some people like more information than others, but as a rule, elaborate explanations are not necessary.

> I like to be told when we are approaching steps, but it's overkill for the sighted person to count the steps and tell me how many there will be.

> Some people are just overly helpful, as in, "Now we are going to be curving toward the left." I appreciate the concern, but I don't really need that much narration when I'm holding onto a person.

Do not forget to watch for obstacles from above. If your companion is taller than you, do a quick mental calibration before strolling under a chandelier or low hanging branch.

If you need to do an about-face, allow her to drop your arm as you turn inward toward her, then let her take your arm again when you are both facing the other direction. Do not attempt a half-circle sweep linked together, a maneuver which consumes the entire sidewalk and can taint your popularity during rush hour.

When you come to a closed door, either open it yourself or place her hand on the knob and let her open it. Then lead the way through the doorway. In the case of a swinging door, tell her which side it is on so she can catch it as she follows.

> I usually like to open my own doors. If someone else opens a door for me, I have trouble knowing exactly when and where to enter. The other day I was going to the rest room at work and my friend said, "I'll get the door!" I waited a second and went ahead. But she hadn't quite gotten it all the way open, and I hit my head on the edge of the door.

When you part company, give your companion a short report on where she is and which way she is facing. She may have lost her bearings while walking with you.

## Guide Dogs

Visually impaired people have used dogs as guides for hundreds of years. In the past, dogs were selected haphazardly for this purpose. Today, carefully chosen animals are trained intensively by professionals before they are allowed to serve as guide dogs.

The skills of individual dogs vary, but in general guide dogs are trained to follow spoken instructions such as "left" or "forward," and to lead the way safely. As they travel, they avoid obstructions, barriers, and hazards. They maneuver through crowds or narrow aisles without bumping into things, and they pause at doors, curbs, or stairs until instructed to proceed. A person using a guide dog has less to worry about and therefore can walk more quickly and confidently than would otherwise be possible.

> My dog is trained to recognize and follow 25 different commands. For example, she can find a doorknob and put her head under it so I can locate it without a lot of fumbling. If I lose my way inside a store or office building, I can say, "Outside," and she will take me to the door through which I originally entered. That way I don't have to drop bread crumbs when I go somewhere.

> The other day, they were putting in new lamp posts near my apartment and an entire intersection was nearly blocked off. My dog found a way through, though it took a long time. She even got us around the water puddles because she knows I don't like them.

When it is not needed, a guide dog stays out of mischief. For example, in a restaurant, it will lie quietly under the table while its owner eats. It will not disturb the other diners as an ordinary pet might.

A person using a guide dog must keep mental track of where she is at all times, so that she can give the dog instructions. The dog may be familiar with certain places, but it does not know the intended destination on any given occasion. It cannot ordinarily plot an overall route without instructions along the way.

> Most people overestimate what a guide dog can do. They think the dog can understand where I want to go and all I have to do is mindlessly follow. I got lost once in a large parking lot, and a woman said to me, "You sure have a dumb dog." I said, "It's not the dog who's dumb, it's me!"

> It's a common fallacy that I can just put the harness on my dog and say, "Let's go to the barber shop," or, "Let's go to my sister's house," and my dog will know where these places are. It's not that simple.

A guide dog is on duty any time it is wearing its harness. At those times, others should take care not to do things that will interfere with the dog's performance.

Do not pet or play with the dog without permission of the owner. Do not touch the harness. While the dog is at work, its full attention must be on its job.

Refrain from feeding the dog. Most owners carefully monitor the diet of their dog and take a dim view of others sneaking tidbits of Danish under the table.

Do not speak to the dog or attempt to give it commands. A guide dog is accustomed to following the instructions of only one person: its owner.

> It confuses my dog if other people try to give her commands. If someone wants me to follow him, he should say, "This way, Henry," and let me command the dog. He shouldn't say, "Here, Fifi!"

> It's dangerous for people to talk to my dog. I've had people call to her from across the street and she's tried to run to them.

Keep your pets away. Guide dogs have been trained to ignore other animals, and they will dutifully resist the urge to chase an enticing squirrel across the lawn. But they may find it hard to contend with the distraction of unleashed dogs and cats taunting them at close range.

Have faith in the dog. Do not call out if the dog seems headed for an obstacle, and do not interfere unless there is a genuine emergency. Perhaps you think your pooch at home would march a person right off a cliff, but rest assured that a trained guide dog operates on a much higher standard.

> The hardest thing for sighted people to do is to trust the dog to do her job. People are always thinking the dog won't see a certain step or pothole, and they grab the harness or yell, "Watch out!" This startles my dog and makes her feel insecure. She takes a great deal of pride in her work and is very sensitive to being reprimanded.

When walking with someone using a guide dog, offer your arm. Some visually impaired people like to walk holding a companion's arm in one hand and the dog's harness in the other. Other people find it awkward to be pulled in two directions at once. To avoid the wishbone syndrome, they will either decline the arm or drop the dog's harness, signaling that the dog is off duty. In the latter case, the dog will walk on a normal leash and follow instead of lead.

> When my dog stops, it takes me a minute to figure out why. I feel for a step or barrier, then I feel for an obstacle hanging from above. If I'm walking with a friend, it's nice if he tells me why the dog has stopped.

While a guide dog can be a wonderful aid in getting around, it is also a big responsibility. It must be fed, cared for, and taken outside every few hours like any other dog. In addition, a guide dog requires a certain amount of ongoing training and discipline in order to keep its skills sharp. For many, the drawbacks outweigh the benefits. Only a minority of the visually impaired people in this country use guide dogs.

### Canes

A long cane can perform many of the same functions as a guide dog. By scanning the ground with the tip of the cane, a person who is visually impaired can locate steps, curbs, and other obstructions in her path. A cane is somewhat less versatile than a guide dog, but then it does not eat as much and is a lot easier to care for.

> I can't travel as quickly with my cane as I could with a dog. A dog can sense where there's going to be a problem and avoid it. With the cane, I have to actually make contact with an object to know it's there.

Some people own both a guide dog and a cane and choose between them as the occasion warrants.

I take my dog to work every day, but I leave her home and take the cane when I go to church because she'd be in the way there. I also try not to take her to parties, where too many people would try to pet and feed her.

I use the cane less often than my dog. I'm 6'8" and overhanging objects have always been a problem for me. The dog steers me away from those. The cane, of course, doesn't. Unfortunately, some people shy away from me when I have my dog; they think a big guy and a big dog are an awesome team.

Some canes can be folded away when not in use. These are especially handy for people who have some vision and only need the cane in dim light or unfamiliar surroundings. The non-folding variety of cane can get in the way when not in use, but it has the advantage of being more stable.

A person traveling with a cane may move slowly and haltingly, but she does not necessarily need help. Do not interfere unless there appears to be some unusual difficulty.

Do not touch a cane without permission. If it is in your way, ask that it be moved. Emphatically, never grab a cane while it is in use.

Once I was in a store and the saleslady, trying to help me find something, grabbed the bottom end of my cane and started pulling me along. It was very disconcerting being towed this way. It would have been far better if she had offered me her arm or simply let me follow the sound of her voice.

If a person touches your feet with a cane, step aside and let her pass. Naturally, watch where you are going in public places so you do not trip over a cane.

Children fall over my cane because they run around without looking where they are going. Adults can trip on it, too. Once a man ran in front of me as he was rushing to catch a bus, and he fell headlong over the cane. He was angry with me, but I had no way of preventing this kind of mishap.

When walking with a person who uses a cane, offer your arm. Some people like to walk using both the cane and a sighted person's arm for guidance; others prefer to either put away the cane or decline the arm.

If I fold away my cane and take someone's arm, I have to depend on that person to tell me about potholes or bumps on the ground. Sometimes they forget and I stumble. So I prefer to walk separately and use my came.

I can move much faster holding a sighted person's arm than I could on my own. I usually keep using the cane as we walk because then I get a better idea of where I'm going in case I have to come back by myself later.

If your companion has not taken your arm, walk closely enough for her to reach over and touch you when she wants to make sure you are still together.

## Streets

People assume that when I'm crossing a street, I automatically need help. Not true. They also assume that after I've crossed the street, I don't need help any more. Not necessarily true. Last week I crossed the street and there was a large maintenance truck at the opposite curb, and I could have used some help finding my way around it.

Streets pose one of the biggest hazards in modern cities, and the thought of having to traverse one without the aid of vision would cause most people considerable alarm. But many visually impaired people cross streets regularly and remain in possession of all their limbs. With much practice, they have learned to pay careful attention to the sounds of the street so they can cross when it is safe to do so.

I'll usually stand at a corner for a minute or two to size up the traffic. I can tell if there's a light or not by listening to the cars starting and stopping.

Some people falsely believe my guide dog can see traffic lights and lead me across when the light is green. Dogs are color blind. I have to listen for traffic patterns, and I tell the dog to go when I hear that the traffic has stopped.

Some streets are more difficult to navigate than others. Most problematic are streets which have high speed limits, those which are noisy, and those which are unfamiliar to the visually impaired person. Corners without street lights pose a challenge. Even worse than no light at all is a light which gives pedestrians only a few seconds in which to hurl themselves across the street.

Rounded curbs tend to confuse me. They make it hard to square myself off with the street and head directly across. Curb cutouts are also a problem. If there's just a slope instead of a definite curb, I can be out in the street before I know it.

I'm especially intimidated by big trucks. They are so loud as they idle, and the noise disorients me.

I have problems in places that allow a right turn on a red light. It's scary to have cars zoom out in front of me when I'm crossing with the light. A lot of drivers don't know that the white cane means I'm blind and can't get out of their way.

If you are walking with a visually impaired person and are approaching a street, or if you happen to see a visually impaired person waiting at a corner, give her any information that seems relevant. Tell her when the light is green. Describe anything unusual in the vicinity, such as an extra high curb or an esplanade in the middle of the street. Offer to let her take your arm as you cross.

> Normally I am with my dog, so I don't need any assistance. I don't want to take someone's arm because if I do, then my dog will start depending on other people and she will lose her skills.

> I can cross the street without help, but if someone offers assistance, I'd be a fool not to accept. Even sighted people get hit by cars.

> If a person has some special reason for offering me help, he should say so. For example, maybe there is a manhole across the street and that's why he's offering to help me. I might decline help, thinking I am in a familiar area and not knowing that somebody dug a hole since the last time I was there.

If she accepts your arm, walk slightly ahead and let her follow; never push her in front of you. Tell her when it is time to step up, step down, or step around some obstacle. Do not leave her until she is safely up the opposite curb.

> If I'm following, then I can tell by the person's body movements whether it's a rough street or there are holes in it. If he takes my arm and shoves me in front, then I'm the one who falls in the hole because I don't know where we are going.

If she declines your arm and you are going her way, you might walk close by, to be available for assistance and assurance in case a semi blasts its horn or a speeding car whips around the corner.

> It's nice if another person just walks beside me. That gives me a little added security but still lets the dog do her job. Sometimes things can come up suddenly, and then I'd like to be able to reach over and take a sighted person's arm.

Before you give a visually impaired person any assistance at an intersection, be sure you understand which street she wants to cross. Do not be the helpful stranger who gallantly escorts her a block out of her way.

## Noise

We blind people rely on sounds to know where we are and what is happening around us. If a single loud noise is drowning out all the others, we are lost. That's the equivalent of a very bright light shining in the eyes of a sighted person so he can't see anything else.

People who are visually impaired depend on auditory cues for much of their information about their surroundings. The sound of a person's voice tells how far away he is standing; the reverberations in a room give an indication of its size; the sounds of traffic tell when it is safe to cross a street.

Loud, extraneous noises present a problem if they mask the important sounds such as voices, echoes, and traffic.

Drilling in the streets is especially bad because I can't distinguish that noise from the traffic noise. I can't cross a street safely when I can't hear the traffic.

As a friend or bystander, you can make life easier for a visually impaired person by taking measures to control loud noises until she has passed or become oriented. For example, shut off a clanging copying machine when she enters your office. Give your power lawn mower a break until she has safely crossed the street. Turn down the reggae when she visits your home for the first time.

Unfortunately, not all noise is controllable. The sounds of nature, large scale construction, or overhead airplanes cannot be regulated, and visually impaired people must simply cope with them. One way of coping is to ask for extra help from sighted friends or passersby.

Rain and snow are a big hindrance because they tend to muffle sounds. Cars slosh water everywhere, and I can't tell where they are or which way they are going. My friends always laugh when I say, "Let me take your arm, I can't hear where I'm going."

While loud, pervasive noises are a problem for visually impaired people, the normal sounds of living impart valuable information. It is not necessary or desirable for bystanders to go into freeze-frame at the appearance of a person who is visually impaired.

One of the biggest favors people can do for me is to keep talking or to continue with their normal activities when I arrive. If I can hear them, I know where they are and can walk around them. In the halls of my office building, people tend to stop talking and stand motionless when they see me. Then I don't know they are there, and I bump into them.

Often when I go to the post office, people stop talking when I enter, and I think the place is empty. My guide dog knows I want to go to one of the windows so she just takes me past everyone and up to the front. Finally someone will shuffle a foot and I'll ask, "Is anyone there?" and six assorted voices will say, "Yes." And I'll say, "Did I just cut in front of you?" and they'll say, "Yes." And I will have to apologize and slink to the back of the line.

## Mail

Reading plays a large role in modern life, and many visually impaired people say that the inability to read is one of the most difficult aspects of their impairment. Some people have mastered Braille, a system of writing in which raised dots on a page represent letters and words. But not all written materials are available in Braille.

Future scientific advances will undoubtedly make reading less of a problem for people with visual impairments. Technology will be developed to rapidly convert written and printed materials into either sound or a tactile medium. Some reading devices of this kind already exist, but they are fairly expensive, difficult to use, and are not yet available to everyone.

For the time being, coping with printed and written materials is difficult or impossible for many visually impaired people. They must rely on others to read aloud to them. Personal mail presents a special problem; a new batch arrives every day, whether or not yesterday's has been dealt with!

At the office I have no trouble because there are plenty of sighted people around to read me my work-related mail. At home it's another matter. I live alone, so I usually just let the mail pile up until I have someone available whom I feel comfortable asking to help me.

I can read my own mail if I have plenty of time. I have enough vision to make out most printed materials and dark, clear handwriting.

I use an Optacon (a reading device) to read my bills and bank statements. If something is hand written, I have to find someone to read it to me.

It depends on how my eyes are that day. Some days I can read large print. A volunteer comes to my house once a week to read me the rest.

When you write a letter to a person who is visually impaired, keep in mind that it might not be read immediately. When it is read, others might see its contents. For private messages or for pressing matters, use the telephone.

Consider sending your message by audiotape rather than in writing. Many visually impaired people greatly appreciate receiving mail in this form because they can enjoy it at their leisure, unassisted, in private.

If you do decide to send a conventional letter, type or write in dark ink. Use simple, solid colored stationary. The more legible your letter, the lower its probability of ending up in a swelling heap of unread mail.

When you are in the position of reading mail to a visually impaired person, either as a friend, volunteer, or employee, always remember to respect her privacy. As you take each new piece of mail, identify it by return address and ask whether you should open it. Read it only after getting the go-ahead. Naturally, maintain proper confidentiality regarding anything you read.

> The most emotionally difficult part of losing my vision was giving up my privacy. If I spend a lot at the department store, I know that the person who reads me my mail will see the bill. Heck, I can't even eat junk food without others knowing it, because other people see my grocery list.

Do not automatically skip over any piece of mail, however unexciting it appears to you. Even a flyer or advertisement might be of some interest; ask if you should read it.

# 13.

## BUSINESS ETIQUETTE

### For Cashiers and Tellers

Most people cannot imagine performing monetary transactions without the aid of their sight. But visually impaired people competently handle money every day. They have learned to recognize coins by their sizes and physical properties. They keep track of paper currency by either folding each denomination differently or by filing the various denominations in different compartments of the wallet. Many visually impaired people manage all of their own cash transactions, and in general, money does not slip through their fingers any more quickly than it does with the rest of us.

As a cashier or teller, you are likely to have a visually impaired customer on occasion. When you do, the most important rule in handling the situation is to deal directly with the customer, whether or not a sighted companion is present.

Speak to a visually impaired person as she approaches your register or window so she will know where you are. If she has already found the proper line, tell her when it is her turn. Lightly tap her on the arm if necessary. Be sure she has heard you before you begin to ring up her items or tend to her business.

> After a meal in a restaurant, I tell my guide dog to head for the door. Usually the cashier is positioned somewhere on the way out, and I can tell where he is by the sound of his voice or the noise of the register. But I've had a couple of embarrassing incidents, where the cashier was very quiet and my dog just led me past him and out the door! She knows her job is to get us out. She doesn't care if I pay on the way or not.

When ringing up items, call out the individual prices and announce the total.

> I get around easily so it is not obvious to others that I can't see well. For example, at a cash register I usually cannot make out the total. If I ask the cashier what the total is, a lot of times he'll point to the register and say, "It's right there."

63

Place the change in the customer's hand rather than setting it down on the counter where she will have to search for it. If your cash register delivers change in a cup, guide her hand to it or tell her where it is. Always give a visually impaired person her own change; do not award the windfall to her sighted companion.

Identify each bill as you hand it to her. It is not necessary to identify the coins.

> It helps if the cashier gives me my money slowly enough that I can put it in the compartments of my wallet. It's hard for me to deal with a heap of money all at once.

Check with your customer before giving her a very large bill. Many visually impaired people prefer to carry several smaller bills instead of a single large one. Even the best of filing systems can occasionally break down, and with all small bills one does not risk inadvertently donating the rent money to the girl scouts.

If a visually impaired customer is paying by check, be aware that her checks might be larger than the standard size and she might use a straight edge to help her write in a straight line. She may have a special identification card in place of a driver's license.

### For Salespeople

> Once I was in a store and a woman started assisting me in my shopping. She was extremely helpful, and I was very surprised when we'd nearly finished and she said, "I'll find you a saleslady." That was the first time I realized that she was just another customer and didn't work in the store.

As a salesperson, the most important thing you can do to serve a visually impaired customer is to identify yourself and let her know you are available to wait on her. Presumably all customers would like this service, but sighted people are in a better position to stalk down some assistance if none appears forthcoming. A visually impaired customer depends on you to take the initiative.

If you recognize the customer as someone who shops in your establishment frequently and is familiar with your stock, tell her about new items that are available. Also tell her about anything that has been recently rearranged in or around your store.

> Yesterday I went to the local shopping center, where I know my way around. Things usually stay pretty much the same there, but that day they were having an outdoor sidewalk sale, and racks of merchandise

were in the walkways. Luckily, the nice manager of one of the stores came out to tell me about it before I discovered it the hard way.

When the customer tells you what she is shopping for, give a quick summary of the available products that might fit her need and their respective prices. If a particular piece of merchandise is on sale, mention that fact, but do not discuss that product to the exclusion of all others.

After the selection has been narrowed down, give a more detailed description of the items being considered. Allow the customer to handle them or view them at close range. Offer to read her any relevant written material, such as the tag describing the fabric content or the description printed on the box.

> A lot of sales people just don't talk enough. Usually anything they can tell me about the product is useful.

If asked, offer your personal opinions on what is becoming or serviceable. But keep the advice low-keyed; understand that her tastes are different from yours.

When the customer has chosen an item for purchase, give her a brief rundown of how it operates. In the case of a garment, read her the care label.

> It's so much better if the salesperson knows his product, especially in electronics. Then he can teach me how to work it. If he doesn't know what he's doing, I am going to go home and not know either.

If you must turn her over to another salesperson to complete the transaction, be sure to inform that person that she needs service.

In a large establishment, it is a nice touch to ask a visually impaired customer whether she needs directions to her next destination within the store. She may not be able to read the directory. Ask if she prefers to take the stairs, elevator, or escalator, and direct her accordingly.

> Once in a department store I asked someone where the elevator was. She misunderstood and showed me the escalator. I took a big step, thinking I was getting into an elevator, and boy was I surprised!

If you are in a position to do so, see that the directory and other signs within the store are in large, clear print.

## For Health Care Professionals

Few people are able to visit a doctor's office or enter a hospital with absolute nonchalance. Most of us experience some weakness in the knees at the idea of being prodded and poked with an assortment of cold and strange instruments. Sighted people have the benefit of being able to get a good look at the cold and strange instruments in advance; people who are visually impaired must deal with an element of surprise. As a health care professional, you can make a visit more palatable for a visually impaired patient by taking the following measures.

Speak to her as she enters your waiting room. Identify yourself as someone who works there so she will not mistake you for a chatty fellow patient. Direct her to a free chair where she can wait.

> Usually people in waiting rooms are so quiet that I don't know where they are, and I bump into them looking for a place to sit. Once I nearly sat down in a woman's lap before she yelled, "Hey!" It would be so much easier if someone would say, "There's a free chair just to your right."

When the time comes, guide the patient to the examining room or her hospital room, and give her a brief description of the layout. If she will need to step onto a stool to get to a high chair or table, offer her an arm on which she can steady herself. Ask what type of assistance is needed, and refrain from providing any services that are not wanted.

> I'm a 38 year old man, and one nurse thought I would need help taking off my clothes! I corrected that notion in a hurry.

In a hospital room, or any room where she will stay for an extended period, be sure the patient knows the way out so she can leave in case of emergency. If she has been led into the room by some convoluted route, her notion of the layout of the building may be hazy.

Each time you enter her room, speak to her and tell her who you are. Even if you are just retrieving an instrument, say hello and let her know what is happening. Tell her when you are leaving again.

> Nurses often forget to identify themselves when they enter a hospital room. It's frightening if people walk into my room and I don't know who they are or what they're doing. It would be so reassuring if they would say something like, "Hello, I'm Mrs. Wilson and I'm going to check your I.V."

Before you touch her body, be scrupulous in describing what you are about to do, what instruments you will be using, and what sensations she can expect to experience. If possible, allow her to touch instruments or to view them at close range before you begin to use them.

> I'm always in suspense in the dentist's chair. I know something is going to get stuck into my mouth sooner or later, but I never know exactly when it will be, what it will feel like, or how long it will be there.

Speak to an adult patient directly when giving explanations and instructions; do not route the information through a sighted companion. Give the patient her own receipts, prescriptions, or other papers, handing them over one at a time and identifying each.

### For Restaurant Employees

The following suggestions for restaurant employees assume that a visually impaired customer is dining alone or with other people who are visually impaired. When there is a sighted member of the party, certain of these recommendations can be relaxed.

Speak to a visually impaired customer as she enters your restaurant, and identify yourself as someone who works there. Let her know when it is her turn to be seated, or, if orders are placed at a counter, her turn to step forward.

If possible, seat her in a reasonably quiet part of the establishment, away from the kitchen. Visually impaired people depend on their hearing to know when the server is near or when the food is arriving. It helps if competing sounds, such as the clanging of silverware, are kept to a minimum. If there is a salad bar or buffet table, try to seat her near it so she will be able to get there without having to wind her way around several tables.

Offer her your arm when showing her to her table, then walk at a moderate pace. If she chooses not to take your arm, check back once or twice as you walk to be sure she has not been lost in the shuffle.

> People don't realize that my guide dog, being so close to the ground, can't see over tables and heads. A lot of times the hostess will say, "Follow me," and disappear into the crowd. My dog and I won't have a prayer of ever finding her again.

When you reach her table, place her hand on the back of her chair. Warn her of anything on the table that she should watch out for, such as burning candles or top-heavy flower arrangements. If there is a relish tray or other snack already on the table, describe it to her. Place bread, salt shakers, and other key items within easy reach.

For a person who has a visual impairment, probably the most difficult aspect of eating out is learning what is on the menu. Hurried restaurant employees, reluctant to take the time to read the menu aloud, sometimes try to speed things up by simply saying, "What do you feel like?" Since the universe of possible menu items is large, this approach generally yields more misses than hits. Take it on faith that the quickest and most efficient course of action is simply to read the menu to a visually impaired customer. Or, consider making menus available in Braille or on audiotape. Remember to read her the prices; most people consider them relevant.

> I have found waiters hesitant to read me the menu. They think it's going to take 15 or 20 minutes. It really doesn't take long at all, especially if they start by reading the categories so I can narrow it down. For example, I might not be interested in appetizers that day.

Before she places her order, let a visually impaired customer know that the kitchen personnel is available to cut the food or make other helpful arrangements. The short ribs jardiniere might take on a new appeal after she learns she will not have to tackle them single-handedly. If the food is being served in buffet style, tell her what is available and direct her to the proper line. Ask if she needs some help in serving herself.

When giving any sort of extra help, be as unobtrusive as possible. Refrain from making an unnecessary commotion or drawing undue attention from the other diners.

Speak up clearly each time you approach the table so she will know you are there and are talking to her. Address her directly when taking her order.

> When I'm in a group and the waiter is taking everyone's order, it is so nice if he taps me on the shoulder and says, "And what would you like, ma'am?" instead of saying, "What does she want?" to someone else as though I weren't even there.

If the restaurant is noisy, a visually impaired customer may not be able to hear you bring the water, coffee, salad, and other items. Let her know each time you bring her something. Do not add hot coffee to her cup without notifying her, and do not fill the cup too full. Tell her about anything unusual in the way the meal is being served. For example, if the vegetables are on a separate plate from the main dish, or the dressing is in a little bowl to the side of the salad, mention that.

Remember that a customer who is visually impaired cannot easily catch your eye or wave you down when she needs you. Check back with her frequently during the course of the meal.

When it is time to bring the check, hand it directly to the customer rather than placing it covertly on the corner of the table. Read her the total, and tell her whether payment should be made to you or to a cashier. If there is a sighted person in the party, do not automatically assume that he will be taking care of the check.

## For Taxicab Drivers

The two most important things my blindness prevents me from doing are reading and driving. Taxis are a way of life for me. They are my major means of getting around.

People who have visual impairments are likely to rely on public transportation for many of their day-to-day needs. As the driver of a taxicab, you can take certain measures to better serve this group of passengers.

When you approach a visually impaired person on the street, speak to her and identify yourself. Do not simply honk from the curb and expect her to come running.

Unless I hear the dispatcher, I can't tell a cab from any other car. I don't want to just get into any car that honks.

Although I always mention that I am blind when I call for a taxicab, the drivers sometimes have the notion that I'm going to be more aggressive when they approach. Once I called a cab and waited 45 minutes on a street corner. It turned out that the driver had been circling that block for a long time, but he kept passing me by because I didn't wave or acknowledge him.

When a visually impaired person is about to enter your car, guide her to the door, open it all the way, and place her hand on the handle. Tell her which way the car is facing. See her into the car before you return to the driver's seat.

Listen as she tells you her destination, and do not discount her directions for getting there.

I sometimes have a hard time convincing a cab driver that, although I am blind, I really do know the way to my house. I live in an out of the way spot, and if cab drivers would just stop and listen to my directions, they would save themselves much exasperation and save me the expense of many circular journeys.

Try to get her as close as possible to her exact desired destination. Do not let her out across the street or around the corner from where she expects to be and assume she will be able to sift things out. At a large public building, drive to the main entrance unless she has specified otherwise.

When you reach the destination, announce your arrival, and if possible, open the door for her. It is a nice touch to help orient her when she gets out and send her off with some brief directions. At an intersection, confirm that you are at the corner she desires. Point out anything unusual about the immediate vicinity, such as a scaffold, mud puddle, or steep curb. If she is headed across a street, tell her whether the light is red or green.

### For Bus Drivers

A bus driver must serve many people and cannot provide the same personal attention as the driver of a taxicab. Still, a few basic courtesies are in order for a passenger with a visual impairment.

If a visually impaired person is waiting at one of your stops, call out your route number as the doors open so she will know whether to step in line or stand back and wait for the next bus. In the event she enters your bus, talk to her as she ascends, and tell her where the coin box is.

When she asks you questions, speak up clearly in response; do not nod or point. It is likely that she will tell you her destination and ask you to inform her when it is time to get off. If the bus is crowded, direct her to an empty seat so she will not have to spend a lot of time looking for a place to sit. Be sure to give her a chance to sit down before you hit the gas pedal. (Not that sighted people should be hurled against the rear window.)

Even if you have agreed to announce her stop, a visually impaired passenger might be concerned about overshooting her mark. For a long trip, call out the names of a few stops along the way; this will reassure her that she is still on course and will dispel her visions of ending up in the depot at the shift change.

> I wish bus drivers would not get impatient when I ask if we're near my stop. If I'd only intended to go a couple of miles and we drive for a half an hour, I get nervous.

As she leaves your bus, mention any obstructions in her direct path. If there is some significant hazard in the vicinity, such as extensive construction work in progress, help her off the bus personally. Give her any necessary directions to subsequent points of transfer.

If a transfer is necessary only because you have neglected to inform her of her intended stop, she is probably in unfamiliar territory. In this case take a more active role in getting her safely to the nearest transfer point. For example, you might ask another passenger to escort her across a busy street to catch a bus going in the opposite direction.

## Written Materials

In the course of daily life, most people exchange various written materials: business cards, meeting notes, forms, and applications. Sighted people are often unsure whether to include a person who is visually impaired in this type of exchange. It might seem foolish to hand a business card or brochure to someone who obviously cannot see. Then again, that person may very much want the information in question and may have the facilities to deal with it in written form.

> Often at meetings, someone will hand out sets of notes and skip me, thinking I can't read them anyway. I don't like getting left out this way. I'd rather they give me my copy and let me get someone to read it to me afterwards.

When in doubt, the safest course is to give the visually impaired person the option to accept or to refuse something in written form. If the person accepts the material, offer to stay a moment and help deal with it.

> I live alone, and anything written on a piece of paper is in danger of getting lost in the shuffle. People hand me a piece of paper with their phone number and say, "Call me sometime," and run off. Then by the time I get home I have three or four pieces of paper and I don't remember what they are. It helps if people have some patience and wait while I write the information down in Braille. Or they could read it to me aloud. I have a good memory.

> Completing forms is always a problem. When I first moved to this city, I was applying for jobs and the clerks would always ask if I could take home the job application and get someone to fill it out for me. Since I lived alone and didn't know anyone in the city yet, this would have been difficult. So it was a big help when they would fill it out for me there at the office.

For written materials that are unusually extensive, see what you can do to pare the task. For example, you might offer to mark relevant passages of a long booklet.

> People don't realize how long it takes to get printed material read. They may hand me a thick book and say, "You can get someone to read this to you, can't you?" The person who reads me my mail will read short things, but finding someone to read me a whole book is not easy.

If you are in a position to do so, consider making commonly used written materials available in another medium. For example, frequently used pamphlets or business brochures can be printed in Braille or recorded on audiotape for the benefit of patrons who have visual impairments.

> It would be extremely helpful if professors would be more verbal in their lectures. Too often, they write on the chalkboard for ten minutes and then say, "As you can see . . . "

# 14.

## CONVERSATION

### Greetings

I like to shake hands. It gives me the feeling of being in contact with the person. Also, it lets me know where he's standing.

You can tell a lot about a person from shaking hands. For example, you can get an idea of his or her height. The voice becomes a real person.

When you first meet a person who has a visual impairment, feel free to shake hands. Many visually impaired people enjoy this custom and routinely initiate it. If you would like to shake hands and the other person has not extended hers, let her know by saying, "How do you do, let me shake your hand." Naturally, the process of aligning and making contact is up to you.

Thereafter, identify yourself each time you see her, until you are told that doing so is no longer necessary. When you are with other people, identify them as well.

People think that once we've met, I will always recognize their voices. That's not true. Some people have an accent or way of speaking that makes them easy to recognize, others don't. Also, the acoustics of a particular place can make a voice sound different from usual.

Since I have some vision, people expect me to recognize them, but often I can't. I especially have trouble when people come to the door. When they stand in the doorway against the glare, all I see is silhouettes. I don't recognize my own children under those circumstances.

When I pass friends on the street, a lot of times they'll say, "Hi," and keep going. I won't have any idea who they are. Then I'll see them later and say, "Gee, I haven't seen you in a long time," and they'll look bewildered and say, "I just saw you yesterday."

### Comings and Goings

I think back nostalgically to the days before carpeting was popular. Then I could hear people walk. Now they come and go, and I never know it.

73

When you enter the presence of a person who is visually impaired, speak to her and let her know you are there. Otherwise she may be unduly jolted when she hears a nearby chair scraping across the floor or a thunderous sneeze from behind. Let her know when you are leaving, even for a minute.

> When people say hi to me in public, it's hard to tell if they're just passing by or staying to talk. Unless they are wearing squeaky shoes or are pushing a grocery cart, I can't hear them move around. I'd feel foolish starting to talk to the air after the person had already left.

If you are in a public place with a visually impaired person and you plan to leave her alone for a while, tell her how long you will be gone. Before you go, guide her to a chair, wall, or post where she can wait comfortably.

> Sometimes when I'm shopping with a friend, he or she says, "I'll be right back," and leaves me for a time. When this happens, I like to stay somewhere out of the way. I don't like to just stand there in the flow of traffic.

When a visually impaired person hears your voice, she might be unsure whether you are talking to her or to someone else. She may opt to err in the direction of silence rather than pipe up in response to a comment intended for another person. To spare her the guesswork, address her by name when in a group or in public. If you do not know her name, stand directly in front of her and begin speaking. You may also gently touch her arm or repeat yourself once or twice.

> It's fine for someone to get my attention by tapping me on the arm or shoulder. But sometimes this makes me jump and then the person is embarrassed for having startled me. I think it's easiest if the person just starts talking, and if I don't respond, repeats himself. By the second time I hear something, I usually have a good suspicion that it's me the person is speaking to.

## Topics of Conversation

Once people realize I am blind, they will usually ask what caused it. Most are satisfied with a brief explanation. Then if they say something like, "You have coped with it well," and drop the subject, I don't feel the worse for having spoken about it.

I don't mind people asking me about my vision. They will understand me better if I tell them about my impairment. It shouldn't be a one way thing; they should be prepared to tell me a little about themselves as well.

Visually impaired people agree that there is no need for others to avoid any particular topic of conversation around them. The subject of visual impairments is perfectly acceptable, provided it is not pursued to the exclusion of all other topics.

Nor is it necessary to go through verbal contortions in avoiding words such as "look" and "see." Trying to eliminate all occurrences of these words from normal speech would be mentally exhausting and would result in some strange phraseology.

> I use these words all the time, and I wish others wouldn't be so shy about using them. I say, "See you later," even though I obviously won't be SEEING the person later. It would sound ridiculous to say, "Hear you later."

Sighted people may feel empathy with a person who is visually impaired, or they may feel admiration for the way she is dealing with her impairment. There is no reason not to express these feelings, on an occasional basis. Empathy and admiration are best received if expressed no more than once or twice within the course of a friendship.

> You don't have to say anything to show compassion. The fact that you are spending time with me shows you care.

> Admiration is okay if it's expressed tactfully, tastefully, and isn't repeated every five seconds. It shouldn't get too schmaltzy.

Humor can put people at ease and foster a sense of camaraderie. Many people with visual impairments enjoy jokes and lighthearted comments about their situation; a few do not. As a rule, jokes coming from friends are more likely to bring smiles than those delivered by strangers.

> I feel more comfortable if my friends can laugh with me. Once in a restaurant, a waitress was concerned that if she stumbled on my guide dog, he would bite her. I assured her that he wouldn't. My friend chimed in, "Yeah, don't worry about the dog. He's used to living with a blind person."

> Once at a fund raising event, I was roller skating around the block with a bunch of other people. My sister was in the crowd watching. I took a spill, and my sister started laughing her head off. Other people in the crowd were horrified that she would laugh at a blind girl. That made her laugh even harder, and she said, "That's okay, she's my sister!"

People with visual impairments have learned to use touch, smell, and hearing to get a sense of their surroundings. Still, many enjoy descriptions from their sighted friends when there are interesting things to see.

When I'm in a new place, it's fun to hear about my environment. For instance, at a restaurant last night, my friend told me about the plants in wicker baskets hanging from the ceiling and the old-fashioned candy jars up on the shelves. That gave me a feel for the place.

A final note: it is not necessary or desirable to speak loudly to a visually impaired person, unless she also has a hearing impairment.

## Candor

Many people have the strange idea that someone puts me together every morning, that I have some sort of full-time personal valet who picks out my clothes, does my hair, and puts on my makeup. Wouldn't that be the life!

Most people put considerable effort into their personal appearance, and visually impaired people are no exception. They are, however, at a disadvantage in evaluating the finished product.

One of the most important things a friend can do for a visually impaired person is to speak up when some aspect of her countenance appears unpremeditated. The sooner she is informed of the matter, the sooner she will be able to rectify it.

My friends understand that I want them to be very frank about the things I need to know. If I mismatch something or overdo my makeup, they'll say, "You look a little too healthy today," or whatever. Even though I've practiced for years, I always worry that today will be the day I really mess up.

Once I wore two different colored shoes for a whole day. I'm sure the people at work noticed, but nobody spoke up. The first person who told me about it was the bus driver on my way home.

The worst thing someone can do is let me go around looking frowzy. Let's face it, I attract attention. People are going to look at me and form opinions about blind people in general. So I always try to look nice, and I expect my friends to tell me if I've missed my mark.

# 15.

## SOCIALIZING

### Making Plans

When a visually impaired person is making plans for a social event, the key issue is likely to be transportation. Public transportation is usually available in cities, but it has its drawbacks. Buses have limited routes and can be slow; taxicabs tend to slenderize the pocketbook. Consequently, invitations to social events are doubly welcome when they are accompanied by offers to provide the transportation.

> I don't want my friends to feel as though they have to pick me up whenever we do things together. So my initial response is always to take a taxi. But if a friend really doesn't mind picking me up, then that is wonderful. A ride with a friend is simpler and cheaper than a cab ride, and of course it's more fun, too.

If an invitation does not include an offer for transportation, a visually impaired person is likely to appreciate some advance notice so she can arrange for a ride.

> I use a special transportation service for people with disabilities. It's convenient and reasonably priced, but it needs to be booked six days in advance.

Provided transportation is not a problem, some visually impaired people prefer to meet with their friends outside the home. Others like to do at least a part of their socializing in their own homes, where the surroundings are familiar.

> The trend is to go to a restaurant or other neutral place with new acquaintances. But I would rather have them to my house. I know where everything is. It's a little much to try to learn about a new person and a new place at the same time.

> I'm the kind of person who loves to get out of the house. I want to socialize anywhere but here.

## Recreation

Some of my friends from church were making plans for an outing to a water park, and they thought I wouldn't want to go along. They couldn't believe it when I told them that I was an avid fan of water parks!

When planning an activity which seems to require vision, sighted people sometimes decide out of hand that their visually impaired friends would not want to participate. They are frequently incorrect.

Visually impaired people enjoy a wide variety of recreational activities, including some that would surprise sighted people.

I love to bowl, and my scores aren't all that bad. I can see well enough to center myself at the end of the lane and roll the ball. Then the people I'm with tell me how many pins I hit.

Many visually impaired people enjoy television, movies, or plays, provided the particular offering is not unusually visual in nature. During passages without dialogue, sighted friends can quietly provide some key details.

Usually in the opening scene of a movie there isn't much dialogue. It helps if a friend describes that scene for me since it generally sets the tone for the rest of the movie.

Special effects are popular these days, and it's nice when a friend leans over and tells me about them.

At a quiet moment on a television program, I love being told about the costumes or hairdos.

Often, the companionship of doing things with friends is at least as important as the activity itself. For example, many totally blind people say they would have fun with a group of sighted friends at a museum, discussing the displays or just chatting.

It's fun to be part of a group. I went to a ballet the other day. I'm sure I missed a lot, but I also got a lot out of it. The music was lovely and I could see some of the action. I couldn't see the costumes, but my friends told me about them.

I enjoy going to baseball games, although I don't see as much as my sighted husband does. We often go with a friend of ours who is totally blind, and I think he enjoys these outings more than either my husband or me. He could obviously listen to the game on the radio at home, but there's a certain excitement to being there.

On the other hand, many visually impaired people do have activities which they cannot enjoy and routinely avoid due to their impairment.

I dislike receptions of any kind. I normally recognize people by the way they act, move, and speak, but at a reception there is so much noise and confusion that I can't focus on any single individual. I may seem to snub someone whom I simply don't recognize.

I've never been able to learn to dance. Maybe if I could see, I still wouldn't be any good at it.

I don't like to go somewhere if there will be absolutely nothing for me to do. For example, if everyone else will be playing volleyball and there won't be anyone on the sidelines for me to talk to, then I won't go.

With so much individual variation in tastes, it would be futile to try to predict what forms of recreation a particular person would or would not enjoy. Our recommendation is as follows: if you are planning a certain activity and you would enjoy having a visually impaired friend along, invite her. Let her decide whether or not she wants to join you. A little enthusiastic encouragement, kept within reason, is acceptable if she seems to be vacillating. But respect her wishes if she chooses to decline.

## Restaurants

When planning a meal out with a visually impaired companion, consult with her before selecting a restaurant; she may have some special requests. For example, she might want to pass over a bustling cafeteria or a place that is unusually noisy. If she has some vision, she may reject a place with a dusky ambience in favor of one with more liberal lighting.

I usually avoid cafeterias. I can't see what's being served, and it's hard to know when it's my turn to order. I can't carry my own tray because I'd bump into something on the way. A regular sit-down meal is so much simpler.

When you arrive at your table, help your companion locate her chair before seating yourself. Alert her to anything on the table that she should watch out for, such as burning candles or tall unstable vases. If there are relish trays, rolls, or other things to eat and drink already on the table, tell her about those as well. Do not consider water and crackers unworthy of mention; while unexciting, they can hit the spot.

For many people, deciding what to order is the highlight of the meal. As you survey the menu, read aloud the various items and their prices for your companion. You might read aloud the category headings first and zero in on the key sections, although some would say perusing the noncontenders is half the fun.

If you are willing to help with the cutting of meats or other difficult foods, offer your services before your companion makes her meal selection. Your offer may make a difference in what she decides to order.

> I can cut my own meat if I have to, but I prefer not to do so in public. I feel awkward about it, and there's always the chance I'll slip and end up with gravy in my lap. So if someone else offers to do it for me, I almost always gladly accept.

When the meal arrives, you might say a word or two about the arrangement of the food on her plate. Some visually impaired people find a brief description helpful, others find it to be of no particular benefit. In any case, if there is something unusual about the presentation of the food, or if the plate houses some purely decorative item that you suspect your companion would not care to eat, by all means mention that fact. If there is a buffet table or salad bar, offer to accompany her through the line or to fix her a plate of food.

> I use my fork to find the various foods on my plate. Vegetables are soft, meat is firm, and so on. But sometimes there's a garnish or something I'm hard pressed to identify. It's nice if a friend says, "There's a huge apple ring on the left side of your plate."

> People think I can see well enough to pick out my own foods at a buffet table. But I find it very helpful if a friend goes with me and describes the various dishes. The other day, I took a big heap of what I thought was mashed potatoes to go with my roast beef. When I got back to the table and started eating, I discovered that it was horseradish.

Help flag down the server if your companion needs something during the course of the meal, but do not attempt to speak for her when he arrives. Simply let her know that the server is present and allow her to make her own requests.

In some circles, sparring for the check at the close of a meal is an obligatory ritual. However, when one member of the party cannot even see the check arrive, let alone make an effective dive for it, a more direct approach is in order. If it is your companion's turn to take care of the check, read her the total, place the check in her hand, and keep the feigned protestations to a minimum.

# 16.

## ENTERTAINING

### Arrival

At my mom's house, there's a straw basket hanging from the ceiling in a narrow hall. I don't know how many times I've knocked that thing down.

When expecting a visually impaired guest to your home, have a quick look around for any obvious hazards or precarious situations. Close the door to the basement. Place burning candles or breakables in a safe spot away from the center of activity. See that cabinet doors are not ajar, especially those at forehead level. Check outside, too, to be sure the kids have not left a stray roller skate strategically positioned on the front porch.

If this is your guest's first visit to your home, give her a short tour when she arrives. Familiarize her with the areas where she will be spending time, and point out the rest room. Tell her about stairs, room dividers, low chandeliers, or other things she should watch out for. Be sure to mention your sunken living room before she takes that first giant step.

> There is the tendency to escort me to a chair and park me there for the duration. I prefer a little tour, so that I can get up and move around without feeling klutsy.

> People who have been to my home tend to think I can see more than I can. They don't realize that I've memorized my surroundings in my own home. I need to learn where things are in theirs.

> I like to be shown where the bathroom is when I get there. That way, I won't later have to interrupt a big intense conversation to ask someone to show me the way.

Tell your guest who is present and introduce her to the people she does not already know. Lead her to a chair where she can sit, and place her hand on the back of it. If refreshments are set out, offer to serve her some.

Warn her if there is a dog or cat in the room so she will not be unnerved when she feels her hand being licked.

> I stayed at a bed and breakfast inn last year and the owner told me that there would be a dog in the house during the night. As it turned out,

the dog restlessly paced the house for hours and even came into my room at one point. I was really glad I had been forewarned and knew what it was. My imagination might have run rampant otherwise!

If your guest has a guide dog, check with her before letting your pets into the room.

My dog is accustomed to living alone with me, and sometimes it's hard for her to adjust to having other animals around. Certain cats have a knack for provoking her.

It's great if someone has another dog and a fenced-in area where the dogs can play. Then I just take my guide dog out of harness and let her romp. If a guide dog has periods of play, she's more eager than ever to get back to work when the time comes.

For a long visit, offer to put out a water dish for the guide dog.

If you have things in your home that you are particularly proud of, show them to a visually impaired guest, as you would to a sighted person. She may enjoy touching them or viewing them at close range, or, depending on the nature of the objects, she may enjoy just hearing about them.

Opinions diverge regarding tours of the rest room. Some visually impaired people like a quick rundown on where to find things; others just like to be shown the proper door and will take it solo from there, thank you. Use your judgement regarding how much to say. If you think your rest room is relatively mundane, it is okay to keep quiet; if your toilet paper is behind a secret trap door, speak up.

I like people to say a word or two about the rest room when I'm about to use it. I want to know if the towel rack is up high or the soap is in a fancy dispenser, and I especially want to know if there is anything breakable that I should watch out for.

One bathroom is pretty much like the next, and I'm more comfortable just figuring things out for myself. Sometimes my host comes in with me and gives me this long drawn out description of the bathroom while I'm standing there wondering if he's ever going to leave.

Some people who are visually impaired prefer to remain fairly sedentary when in a strange place; they do not like to move about without guidance. Others like to venture forth and learn about the surroundings on their own.

I asked a friend if it was okay if I walked around and explored the house, and she said, "Yes, provided you take a dust cloth!"

People are often surprised when I offer to help in the kitchen. They think that because I am blind, there isn't anything I could possibly do to help. They don't seem to realize that I cook every day.

For an overnight stay, show your guest around her quarters. Demonstrate the use of the shower, thermostat, bathroom heater, or any other appliance that she may have occasion to use. If there is a telephone in her room, point it out. Be sure she knows how to reach an exit in case of emergency and how to come join you in the morning.

I like to be able to emerge on my own in the morning, without someone having to come find me.

Warn her of any unusual happenings that she can expect during her stay. For example, if children might be getting up during the night, or if the wind on your weather vane sometimes sounds like a cat being strangled, prepare her for that.

First and foremost, I'd like my host to relax. Now and then someone will hover over me and worry about my every move. That's not necessary at all.

### Serving Meals

At every banquet I ever go to, there they are. Cornish hens. You're not supposed to pick them up with your fingers, and they positively defy my efforts with the knife and fork.

As a rule, anything which is difficult to eat with the aid of vision is even more difficult to eat without it. If you are preparing to invite a visually impaired person for a meal, particularly a formal meal, try to plan a menu which will not pose any unusual challenge.

It's hard to cut something round and slick like a tomato. Eating a stuffed tomato is like trying to eat a billiard ball.

A blind person's nightmare is spaghetti.

Salads can be a mess if the lettuce is not cut up well. Those big floppy leaves are so awkward. I tell people that when I eat a salad, they need to run for cover.

Any food is difficult to eat if the plate is too full. When serving food to a person who is visually impaired, allow some space on the dish for maneuvering. Leave a little extra room at the top of a glass or cup.

Let her know what foods and drinks are being served, and give her a quick rundown of how things are arranged on her plate. If there is anything unusual about the way the food is being served, be sure to mention that. Tell her whether drinks are hot or cold.

> Once I was eating a piece of cake at a function, and there was some sort of flower on it as decoration. I had it on my fork and was about to put it in my mouth when someone spoke up.

If serving dishes are being passed around, or if there is a separate buffet table, ask her if she would like you to prepare her plate for her.

> It takes me a long time to serve myself at a buffet table, and I always worry that I'm slowing down the other people. Also, I never know how much to take because I can't see how much food is available or how much other people are taking. It's so much easier if my hostess fixes my plate.

Offer to help cut meats, remove rind from fruits, or do whatever is necessary to make the meal easier to manage. It is fine to do this preprocessing in the kitchen before serving, but always remember to ask first whether this type of assistance is wanted. Do not just automatically serve a visually impaired person a minced version of the meal everyone else is having.

Let her know if second helpings are available. She may be reluctant to ask for more when she does not know how much is left or how many people are already eyeing it.

### Parties

> It's hard for me to join a group and start talking. I can't catch someone's eye, and I don't want to just interrupt a conversation.

As a host at a large party, the most important thing you can do for a visually impaired guest is to provide some introductions and help her start mixing. Take her to a few people at a time and initiate some conversations; do not simply reel off the names of everyone present as she sets foot in the room and then send her off to mingle.

> I like to be introduced to people at close range so I can get an idea of what they look like.

> A general introduction to a large group isn't so good for me. It helps if I can go meet people individually, shake their hands, and hear their voices.

If she already knows some of the other guests, help her find them. She may have trouble recognizing their voices in a crowded room.

Some visually impaired people like the host to mention their impairment when making introductions; others do not. Until you know an individual's preference on the matter, the safest course is to simply offer standard introductions and omit any reference to the impairment.

It's so much easier if the person introducing me explains that I am blind. Otherwise, the other person might start pointing or say, "Come over here," and I won't know where "here" is.

I don't like a host to introduce me to someone and add, "She's blind." Not only does that make me feel self-conscious, it's not entirely true. I do have some vision. People get terribly confused if they're told I'm blind and then they see me reach for an appetizer.

Ask your guest if she would rather sit down right away or stand for a while. If she wants to sit, find her a chair and place her hand on the back of it.

I want my host to allow me to stand up and socialize rather than sitting me down and rotating people past me. I feel silly being the only one at a party who is sitting down.

Tell her what refreshments are available, and offer to help serve her. She may find it difficult to juggle plates and cups on her own, especially if she is also carrying a cane. Check back now and then to see if she needs refills.

# 17.

## VISITING

I like to have people over to my house. I think it's especially important to have new friends over, so they can get used to me and see that my house is the same as theirs. Usually, once a person has been to my home, he relaxes more with me and doesn't try to do things for me as much.

Many visually impaired people enjoy entertaining, and most say that they do not want their guests to take their impairment into any special account. Still, there are a few things a sighted guest can do to make his visit as pleasurable as possible for all concerned.

If you are a close friend, offer to come to a party a few minutes ahead of the other guests, to take a quick look around. A person who is visually impaired might feel more confident if a sighted friend gives the place a clean bill of health before the festivities get underway.

When I have sighted people over, I find myself wondering whether I missed a spot vacuuming or left the dust rag draped over the piano.

During the visit, keep your belongings in predictable places; do not leave a purse on the floor or a pair of reading glasses where your host might sit on them. Avoid inventive resting spots for your half-full glasses or plates. If you move something breakable from its usual spot, inform your host.

Feel free to offer help in the kitchen, but proceed with some prudence. Be sure to get exact instructions of what needs to be done, and avoid improvisation. Try not to rearrange things unnecessarily; putting cinnamon where your host expects the pepper may spell the death of the stroganoff. Keep breakables away from the center of activity. Do not set anything down on the stove. Your host might turn it on later, not realizing something is on it. Keep cabinet and pantry doors either all the way open or completely closed; do not leave one ajar where it will catch your host in the shin.

I can manage most things by myself, but there are a few jobs I ask guests

86

to do. I'm not very good at cutting a pie into neat little pieces, for example.

It's nice if people help me clear the table because, let's face it, I'm slow. If they give me a summary of where they've put things, I won't have too many surprises later.

Speak up if you need something during the course of the visit. All hosts want their guests to be happy, but visually impaired hosts cannot tell when coffee cups are empty or guests are gazing longingly in the direction of the cookie plate.

Guests in my home need to take some initiative in making themselves comfortable. I can't see their expressions, so I don't know if something's wrong unless they tell me. If they're cold, they shouldn't subtly hunch their sweater around their shoulders. They need to say, "Sheila, I'm cold, turn up the heat."

Check with your host before lighting a cigar or cigarette so she will not have to speculate on what it is she smells burning. If your host is also smoking, take care not to pull away an ashtray she is using without telling her. Make sure your butts are completely extinguished when you are finished.

Before you depart, look around and be sure you have not scrambled your host's belongings beyond redemption. Spare her the effort of hunting things down after you have gone; retrieve the tea cup on the window sill or the wine glass you stashed on top of the china cabinet. Take special heed in the kitchen or the bathroom, where items are likely to be meaningfully arranged. Replace what you have moved so your host will not be brushing her teeth with tile cleaner tomorrow morning.

# 18.

## CHILDREN

One of the lesser joys of parenthood is hearing one's child make a loud, blunt comment about a nearby person whose appearance or manner is unusual. The best way to prevent such a potentially awkward situation is to give the child some advance preparation.

Familiarize your child with the spectrum of human abilities and disabilities. With regard to visual impairments, explain to him that some people cannot see as well as others, and that these people learn to rely on their other senses. If the child is young, help him understand by having him don a pair of sunglasses fogged with petroleum jelly; let him learn to do one or two simple tasks without the aid of clear vision. Tell him about any people in your circle of acquaintances who are visually impaired.

> I expect my sighted friends to tell their children that I am blind. Otherwise a child might notice something amiss but not know what's wrong and just shrink from my company.

Even the most diligent attempts at educating your child cannot ensure that he will behave with grace and discretion on all future occasions. When faced with the actual presence of a visually impaired person, he may well position himself in easy earshot and express his renewed curiosity in his best megaphone voice. Since it is probably futile to pretend he is not your child, you have two options in such a situation: you may either offer the necessary explanations yourself or refer the child's questions directly to the visually impaired person. In the latter case, it is your responsibility to monitor the conversation. A child can sometimes pursue a line of questioning with astounding perseverance; if several questions have been asked and answered and no end is in sight, step in and suggest that the interrogation be brought to a close.

> I think it is important that children be educated about blindness so I don't mind taking time out to answer their questions. I know more about the subject than the sighted parent. Most kids are curious about my guide dog. So I explain how she helps me, and then I let them pet her. That always makes a hit.

Section Three

# ETIQUETTE WITH PEOPLE WHO HAVE HEARING OR SPEAKING IMPAIRMENTS

# 19.

## SOME PRELIMINARIES

I was with a friend in an airport cafeteria, and we got to talking about my hearing loss. I made him a bet that, right in that room of maybe three dozen people, there were at least two other people who were deaf. He looked around, decided it was a pretty ordinary-looking group, and bet me $20. I hadn't gone to half the tables before I was $20 richer!

The most invisible groups of impairments are those which affect hearing and speech. Most people do not realize how common these impairments are because they are not apparent to the casual observer.

Part of the frustration of my problem is that no one can see it. I wish people were more aware that not everyone has good hearing. Then they would not be so quick to take offense when they come up and talk to me and I don't answer.

A hearing-impaired person may have a decreased ability to hear sounds, or he may not be able to identify the sounds he hears. The impairment may be slight, moderate, or so severe that he has no usable hearing at all. Many people are helped by hearing aids, but these devices do not necessarily eliminate the problem altogether. Other people are not helped at all by the hearing aids currently available.

A lot of people think, "If you can't understand me, go get a hearing aid." If only it were that easy! It's the nature of my impairment that spoken words sound mushy to me instead of distinct. Hearing aids magnify sounds. Instead of regular sounds that I don't under-stand, a hearing aid would give me louder sounds that I still didn't understand.

Speaking impairments cause more confusion than hearing impairments because they take so many forms. A speaking-impaired person may have difficulty speaking loudly enough, quickly enough, fluently enough, or clearly enough. He might find speaking to be tiring. He may use an artificial larynx, a device which helps generate speech. His voice may have an unusual sound. Or, he may not be able to speak at all.

91

Everyone experiences some sort of vocal fatigue from time to time: hoarseness, laryngitis, stuttering, shaky voice. So when people encounter an unusual voice such as mine, they automatically assume it's a temporary aberration. It is not.

Both hearing and speaking impairments interfere with everyday communications. These kinds of impairments can therefore be called "communication impairments."

A common misconception about communication impairments is that hearing impairments and speaking impairments always go hand in hand.

When I first began having trouble with my voice, I would communicate with people by writing them notes on a piece of paper. I was surprised at how many people assumed that, since I couldn't speak, I naturally couldn't hear either. They would yell to me, or invent their own sign language, of which I knew nothing.

I lost my hearing as an adult, so of course I already knew how to speak. Strangers sometimes don't believe me when I tell them I am deaf, because I speak so well. It's beyond me why I'd want to pretend to be deaf if I weren't!

In fact, most people with speaking impairments have normal hearing. Many people with hearing impairments have excellent speech skills, especially those whose hearing impairment is not severe or not of long standing.

On the other hand, since people commonly learn to speak by listening, some hearing-impaired people do not have strongly developed speech skills. Their speech may be difficult for others to understand, or they may not speak at all, relying exclusively on other means of communication. In a broad sense, these people can be considered speaking impaired as well as hearing impaired.

# 20.

## INITIATING COMMUNICATION

Some communication-impaired people converse, using speech and hearing, in spite of their impairment. Others use additional methods of communication part or all of the time.

I'm hard of hearing, but with my hearing aid, I can still get the gist of most conversations.

With other deaf people, I usually use sign language. With hearing people, I always start out trying to speak and lipread. Then if we have trouble understanding each other, which happens a lot, I write things down on paper and ask them to do the same.

I speak until my voice gets too tired, then I write. I know sign language but don't have much opportunity to use it since none of my friends know it.

Lipreading (or "speechreading") is the ability to understand speech by watching mouth movements. Not all speech sounds are visible on the lips, so lipreading involves observing the visible sounds and using skillful guesswork to fill in the blanks. Some hearing-impaired people are adept at lipreading; others are not comfortable with the method. Lipreading is most effective when combined with partial hearing.

Sign language and fingerspelling are two methods of communication which employ the hands. With fingerspelling, each letter of the alphabet is represented by a certain hand symbol, and words are spelled out. With sign language, or "signing," entire words and phrases can be expressed with a single hand symbol. Sign language and fingerspelling are usually used together; certain words, such as names, are fingerspelled, while others are signed. Many hearing-impaired and a few speaking-impaired people are skilled at this type of communication.

Since almost all adults are able to read and write, people with hearing or speaking impairments usually have the option of communicating on paper. This method is slow, but it gets the job done.

Without thinking, almost everyone uses gesture, body language, and facial expression as a means of communicating. Most people with speaking or hearing impairments pay special attention to using and observing such non-verbal messages.

When initiating a conversation with a person who has a communication impairment, our advice is as follows: begin by asking him, orally or in writing, how best to communicate.

> When they learn I am deaf, most people immediately ask, "Can you lipread?" But often they don't really understand what lipreading entails. They will want to talk to me while looking down at paper and expect me to understand, or the light may be too dim for me to see their lips clearly. Rather than saying, "Can you lipread?" it would be more to the point if they said, "What is the best way for us to communicate?" Then I could say, "Let's move to a spot with more light," or whatever.

Do not despair if communication is difficult at first. With just a little patience and experimentation, things can look up pretty quickly.

> Sometimes I begin speaking, and I can see from the other person's panicked expression that he's thinking, "My god, I can't understand this guy!" But usually in a very short time, he's tuned in to my voice and we're having a conversation.

# 21.

## TALKING WITH A HEARING-IMPAIRED PERSON

### Getting His Attention

*I really have to concentrate to hear and understand what is being said to me. Sometimes a person starts speaking before I see him and before I am mentally connected. Then I'm behind right from the start of the conversation. It takes me a minute to tune in.*

The first step in communicating with a hearing-impaired person is getting his attention. Do not begin a conversation until he has noticed you and is prepared for it.

To get his attention, stand in front of him and say his name. If a person can hear any speech at all, his own name is usually the easiest sound to recognize. Speak up, but resist the temptation to shout.

*Sometimes at work people scream at me to get my attention. This doesn't bother me, since I'm totally deaf, but it bothers other people so I wish they wouldn't do it.*

If the person does not respond to his name, tap him lightly on the arm or shoulder. Or, if you are not within touching range, wave your hand and try to make contact visually.

*Some people feel it's intrusive to touch me while I'm working, and they go to great lengths to avoid it. I'll be leaning over my drafting board and they'll scrunch down and poke their head between me and the paper to get my attention. It's really much easier just to tap me on the shoulder.*

You can also try getting his attention by knocking on his desk or rapping on a wall near him. Many hearing-impaired people have trained themselves to notice the vibrations generated by this kind of thumping.

Turning the lights on and off a couple of times will almost certainly get his attention. Unfortunately, it will get everyone else's as well. Use the light switch when you and he are alone; otherwise, use a method with greater selectivity.

## Position for Speaking

Many hearing-impaired people can understand a certain amount of speech. How much they understand in any given situation depends, to a great measure, on the speaker. When you are with a hearing-impaired person who has indicated that speaking is the best way for you to communicate, a few actions on your part can make things go more smoothly. The first step is to position yourself correctly before you begin.

Remember that the person is understanding you through partial hearing, lipreading, or a combination of the two. Therefore, your objective is to position yourself so that your mouth is clearly visible and your voice carries well.

Face your listener squarely. Do not look down or turn your head in the course of speaking. Naturally, never turn your back to him, a move which muffles the voice and reduces to zero a lipreader's chance of absorbing anything you say.

> With my hearing aid, I can hear some speech, but I also have to lipread if I'm going to follow the conversation. Sometimes people talk into my ear, thinking that this helps me understand. Actually, I understand almost nothing when they do that.

Do not try to speak with something in your mouth. Eating, smoking, or chewing gum affects both the sound of your voice and the appearance of your lips. Keep your hands away from your mouth while you speak.

If you have a beard or mustache which obscures your lips, accept that a hearing-impaired person will have a more difficult time understanding you. Since you would probably consider it extreme to shave for the occasion, try to compensate by paying extra close attention to the other suggestions set forth.

Position yourself with the light source behind your listener so that the light falls on your face.

> Lighting is extremely important to me, since I am trying to see the lip movements and the facial expressions. Light from behind the speaker is hard on my eyes. It highlights the outline of the head but not the features.

When possible, stay three to four feet away from your listener. Farther away, and your mouth movements will be less visible to him and your voice less clear. Closer, and he will get a kink in his neck trying to look at you. Do not even think about talking to him from another room.

If a tall person stands too close and starts speaking to me, I have to look straight up and I can't read his lips. This problem arises in elevators and other cramped areas.

It's true that it's hard to read lips from too far away, but mostly I have the opposite problem. People think they are doing me a favor by coming right up close to me. I prefer just a normal conversation with the person a few feet away, so I can see his face without having to cross my eyes.

## Speaking

Most people with hearing impairments find some voices easier to understand than others. For example, many do better with men's voices than women's, which are higher pitched. Almost all have an easier time understanding native speakers than people with foreign accents. While you cannot do much to improve upon your gender or place of origin, you can take several other measures to boost the intelligibility of your speech. If you are with a hearing-impaired person who understands speech, the following guidelines will help you do the best you can with the raw materials you possess.

Speak moderately loudly, but do not shout; shouting makes words sound less distinct and tends to contort lip movements. Maintain your speech at a uniform volume. Take care not to drop your voice at the end of a sentence, since the last two or three words can be the most important.

Talk a little more slowly than usual, especially if the hearing-impaired person is not yet familiar with your voice and way of speaking. Pause slightly at the end of a sentence, to allow time for your remark to sink in. Pause an extra moment when you are about to embark upon a totally new topic of conversation.

If someone just starts a new subject out of the blue when my mind is still on the last one, I might be lost for a while. It helps if I have a moment to put things into context.

My lipreading comprehension is 35%, which means I catch about one word out of three. You'd be surprised what I can do knowing one word out of three if I have some time to think about what the missing words might be. The sentences, "Would you please pass the morning paper," and, "Would you please pass the salt and pepper," look very similar on the lips. But if I have a second to think about it and see that the paper is right by me and the speaker isn't eating anything that requires salt and pepper, I can figure it out.

Make an effort to speak clearly and pronounce every syllable. Move your lips normally; do not exaggerate your mouth movements since doing this distorts sounds and actually makes lipreading more difficult.

> A lot of times I'll tell someone I'm hard of hearing and ask him to speak loudly and slowly, and he'll say, "O–K–A–Y," (loudly and slowly) and then go back to mumbling. That doesn't help me much!

Do not be overly brief, in the belief you are making less work for the listener. Fuller explanations, with a certain amount of redundancy, are easier to understand than short, clipped sentences. Where appropriate, use some examples to help make your point.

When conveying a lengthy message, get some intermediate feedback along the way, to be sure your listener is understanding you. That way, if he does miss a beat, you will have an idea of where you lost him and how far you should backtrack.

> The other person might say "blah blah" died, and I won't know if it's his mother, brother, or pet otter, and I won't want to say anything until I've figured it out. So I might get really behind in the conversation.

If you are asked to repeat something, reiterate verbatim once or twice. After that, rephrase your message; this tactic meets with far greater success than the instinctive action of repeating the same words over and over at increasing decibel levels. Often, breaking a complex sentence into a couple of shorter ones will help.

> I almost always understand something the second time I hear it. I guess it's like the old saying that first you have to hit a mule over the head to get his attention, then you can talk to him.

> There may be a single word in a sentence that is confusing for me to lipread. Usually it's a one-syllable word. For example, the words "back" and "bank" look similar on the lips. If people are imaginative and use a synonym, then I can usually get past that word.

If a single short word is causing the problem, try spelling it aloud. Do not spell aloud a very long word; by the time the person understands every letter in a long sequence and mentally assembles them to form the word, he will probably have forgotten the original sentence.

If you must leave for a moment to answer the door or telephone, let him know what is happening. He may not have heard the bell and may be baffled by your abrupt departure mid-sentence.

Listening and lipreading can be tiring for a person who is hearing impaired. Try not to run your listener ragged with a protracted monologue;

alternate speaking and listening. In a long conversation, ask him if he would like to take a breather now and then.

> I've only been deaf for three years, so I'm still learning. I always tell people, "Please don't be inhibited in talking to me. If I don't get something the first time, repeat it, rephrase it, and if I still can't get it, spell it, write it down, bring out the slide projector, whatever it takes!"

## Writing

Sometimes people start talking to me, but when they realize I'm deaf, they clam up. I always have a pen and paper ready and ask them to write. Although I can lipread a little, writing is really the best way for me to understand them.

In some situations, the most efficient way to make yourself understood is to write down a single word, a sentence, or an entire message. A person who does not hear or lipread will very likely request that all your communication be in writing. A person who does understand some speech may appreciate a written version of a word or words he is having trouble with; in particular, he may prefer to see in writing any piece of information that is important, such as an address, flight time, or name of a medication.

> A lady who works in my office comes from the Philippines, and she is very difficult for me to understand. So whenever I don't get something she says, she writes it down. That way we can still communicate, and we have been able to become friends.

When you write a message to a person who is hearing impaired, pay attention to your handwriting. Having said something that the person was not able to understand, do not compound the problem by presenting him with a note that he is not able to read!

Be creative in using pen and paper; you need not restrict yourself to written words. Often a map, picture, or diagram can do the job twice as well.

Watch his facial expression as he reads your message, just as you would normally watch the face of a person you are speaking to. His expression will give you an indication of whether he is understanding your message and, if so, how he is reacting to it.

## Gestures and Facial Expressions

A simple gesture along with spoken words can help me understand things more easily. For example, a person might say, "That was hard work!" and make a motion of wiping his brow. That gesture would help me know I understood the words correctly.

For people who are hearing impaired, gestures and facial expressions can be invaluable aids in understanding. People who do not hear or lipread rely heavily on these visual cues. Those who do understand some speech still depend on gestures and expressions, for additional information about the content of a spoken message and the emotion behind it.

"Lipreading" is actually a misnomer. "Speechreading" is more accurate. I don't just look at lips when I want to understand a person. I look at his entire face, his expressions, the position of his body, his arm movements. A smile, a frown, or twinkle in the eye can give meaning to words.

Since I can't hear the tone of voice, I often rely on gestures to tell me whether something is being said in earnest or in a comical way. Someone may say, "Oh, I forgot!" and hit his forehead. That lets me know the situation is not serious.

You can tell whether a person is asking a question or making a statement by the look on his face. The words on the lips may be the same in both cases, but the facial expression will be different.

Gestures and facial expressions are a natural part of communication; you doubtless use them to some degree, without conscious effort. But by observing a few guidelines, you can use this non-verbal form of communication to the maximum advantage in a conversation with a hearing-impaired person.

Remove dark glasses and large floppy hats so that your entire face is visible. The eyes are an especially expressive part of the body; allow your listener to see them.

Maintain a natural and relaxed manner; do not strain to exaggerate. Facial expressions and body movements need not be large-scale to get a point across. Sometimes just a glance in a certain direction can communicate more than an unbridled pantomime. Overblown gestures are definitely inappropriate in a public place, where they would kindle the curiosity of bystanders and attract unwelcome attention.

Recognize the limits of gesture alone. Without verbal communication, intuitive body movements and facial expressions cannot accurately convey lengthy or complex messages. When trying to get across complicated information, or anytime gestures alone do not seem to be cutting the mustard, use speech or writing also.

When speaking and using gestures, take care that your body movements have some correlation with what you are saying. Random motions keep your listener off balance trying to sift the bona fide clues from the red herrings.

> Purposeful gesture is almost always helpful. But if people just move their arms around in the air without any rhyme or reason, that's distracting and confusing.

Do not allow your enthusiasm for gesture to override your attention to articulate speech. Remember to keep your hands away from your mouth so that your lips remain continuously visible. Do not move your head about, and do not use so much facial expression that your mouth movements become distorted.

> Gestures are useful, but people should realize that they still have to speak clearly for me to understand them. Sometimes people get so carried away gesticulating that they start mumbling and speaking too quickly. I end up understanding less than I would have without the gestures!

## Surroundings for Speaking

For a person who is hearing impaired, the easiest place to have a conversation is in a quiet room with good acoustics. All types of noise are a hindrance, some more than others. Constantly changing sounds, such as music, interfere the most; low, steady sounds, such as the hum of an air conditioner, intrude the least.

> I'm an avid bowler, but the noise of the bowling alley makes it impossible for me to hear what anyone's saying. One of my teammates told me that the others thought I was unfriendly because I never talked to anyone during the game.

> Rooms with lots of resonance, like gymnasiums or large public rest rooms, seem noisy even when they're empty. It's hard for me to understand what a person is saying when all those echoes are muffling the words.

> The car is my least favorite spot to hold a conversation. Between the engine, the outside wind, and the radio, there's too much noise for me to hear what people are saying. And of course, if I'm the one doing the driving, I can't watch someone's lips.

When a person is depending partially or completely on lipreading, good lighting is essential. A place that is lit brightly and evenly, without a lot of strong shadows, provides the best environment. Light colored walls are also helpful.

For a hearing-impaired person, trying to understand takes effort and concentration. It is difficult to listen and lipread while engaged in another activity or when nearby distractions are demanding attention. The ideal conversation is held sitting down. Conversing while walking down the street is inconvenient; in trying to juggle his gaze between the speaker and the path ahead, the hearing-impaired person invariably misses the crux of the discussion and lurches up a number of curbs.

> I normally understand quite well by lipreading. But if there is a lot of commotion, I just can't focus on the person's lips. For example, in a nightclub, where lights are flashing and people all around are getting up and down, I have a very hard time.

If you are spending time with a hearing-impaired person, do not wear him out by trying to have a discussion when conditions are poor. At the minimum, wait until the band takes a break, the lights come up, or the honking cement truck has rounded the corner. And do not forget that you can write things down in the meantime. Never continue speaking if it is clear the other person is not understanding you.

### Talking in Small Groups

> The people where I work are always confused that I understand them while we are working but not at breaks. In the course of the job, people talk to me individually so I can concentrate on their voice and watch their lips. But at breaks, they sit in groups, the discussion bounces around, and I can't follow what they're saying. By the time I've figured out one topic of conversation, they're off on something entirely different.

> When there are several people talking, I never know who is going to speak next or whose lips to watch. I miss half of what is going on, and it can be embarrassing. I'll be sitting around with three people, and one will say, "Do you want to go to lunch?" and another will say, "Sounds good," and another will say, "Where should we go, maybe an Italian place?" and halfway through I'll suddenly say, "Hey, I have an idea, let's go to lunch!"

Group conversations tend to progress quickly, often without much focus or direction. A hearing-impaired person, even one who normally understands quite well, can easily be left in the dust.

To help him participate, allow him to position himself so that he has a good view of everyone in the group. A frontal view is best because it is difficult to read lips from the side. Two or three people talking to a hearing-impaired person should sit or stand directly across from him. This formation can be modified somewhat with a larger group, so he does not feel like he is on trial, but the same principle applies. In a car, allow him to sit in the front passenger seat, where he can turn around and see the lips of the people in back.

> At church, when people break up into groups after the service, I have trouble joining in. People stand around in circles so that there are always some people in the group that I can't see well.

> If I'm talking to two people, it's so much easier if they stand together opposite me. That way I don't have to keep swiveling my head to one side and the other.

Slow down your pace, and make a concerted effort to speak one at a time. Include the hearing-impaired person in the discussion, and get some feedback on whether he is following the conversation. If the topic at hand is zigzagging and he suddenly looks confused, you might say a word or two to help him catch up. A simple statement such as, "We are talking about lunch," can get him back on course.

> My friends are very sensitive to my hearing problem. If a bunch of them are talking, they'll zero right in on a perplexed look on my face and say, "Are you still with us, Terry?"

> It's hard to get people to speak one at a time. Sometimes I feel like cutting in and saying, "Hey, wait your turn!"

When you are directing a remark specifically to him, be sure to look at him. If he hears his name and looks up to see all members of the group surveying their fingernails, he may be in the awkward position of not knowing who is speaking to him.

> In a group, eye contact becomes so much more important than in a one-on-one conversation. When I'm sitting with several people, I have to constantly scan their faces so I can tell when someone is starting to speak to me. Then I can concentrate on that person and make sure I understand what he is saying.

# 22.

## TALKING WITH A SPEAKING–IMPAIRED PERSON

### Listening

*If a person looks directly at me, if he has a smile on his face or a warm look in his eye, then that encourages me to keep on talking. But if he looks at me strangely or looks away, I feel like I should keep it short.*

Many speaking-impaired people communicate with speech in spite of their impairment. Some of these have normal hearing. Others are hearing impaired; they have learned to speak without the benefit of hearing what speech sounds like, and consequently their speech may sound unusual or may be difficult to understand. The following suggestions apply to both groups of people.

When talking with a speaking-impaired person, accept that the conversation will not move along as rapidly as usual; do not try to rush things. A person who is speaking impaired may speak slowly. One who is also hearing impaired has the additional task of trying to understand your end of the conversation, which takes time.

Face him and maintain easy eye contact. Give the conversation your full attention. In a setting with surrounding noise, move in close to him so he will not have to raise his voice unnecessarily. Do not talk to him from another room or shout to him from a distance and expect him to answer.

Pause for a moment after he says something, to be sure he is finished. Then, speak moderately slowly yourself. If he is speaking for a while, nod now and then, or interject a few words to let him know you are still listening and understanding.

*It seems more like a normal conversation if the other person talks at about the same speed as I do. It's awkward if the dialogue seesaws between me stuttering laboriously and the other person jumping in and trying to make up for lost time.*

Ask him to repeat himself when you do not understand something. Emphatically, do not remain silent, nodding weakly and hoping to make

104

sense of the conversation as you go along; accept on faith that this strategy does not work.

Let him know if there is something he can do to help you understand him. For example, if he is hearing impaired and does not realize that the background noise is drowning him out, ask him to speak up.

Repeat back key pieces of information, such as names or phone numbers, to be sure you have understood them correctly.

> I do best with kids because they're straightforward and they don't worry about hurting my feelings. Sometimes I'm talking to an adult, and he's shaking his head yes, but I can tell by his facial expression that he's probably not understanding a word I'm saying. A kid would never do that. He'd just say, "I can't understand you," and let me say it again.

Alternate speaking and listening. Do not barrage him with one question after another, volleying the ball back to his court each time he takes a breath. Make the conversation two-way, and allow him some moments of respite. Accept that you are not going to learn his entire life story in one sitting.

> Meeting people is hard. Some people have the idea that it's egotistical to talk about themselves so they ask a lot of questions. "Where do you live? What do you do for a living? Are you married? Do you have any kids?" I've barely managed to answer one and they're already asking the next one. It's overwhelming.

Unless you know him well, listen to his words and not to the way he is saying them. Try not to draw conclusions based on his tone of voice or manner of speaking because these may be misleading with a speaking-impaired person.

> I don't have the ability to put inflection or emotion into my voice. Sometimes people think I'm mad when I'm not. Terrible misunderstandings have occurred because of this.

> My speech is slurred, and over the phone people often think I'm drunk. They won't take me seriously, and that's disheartening.

It may be tiring for him to speak; keep your conversation of moderate length unless encouraged to continue. Understand that, for the sake of practicality, he may want to stick to the business at hand and dispense with friendly, non-substantive banter.

> People are often surprised to hear that talking is an effort for me. Since I can't hear myself, I have to concentrate on forming every word

correctly and on not getting too loud or quiet with my voice. After a while, I'm definitely ready for a break.

Most people experience some variation in their impairment. Speaking may be more difficult when one is not rested, not feeling well, or not mentally prepared to talk. The person who seemed to be speaking quite well at your business meeting this morning may not be eager to talk at all when you run into him at the convenience store tonight. Do not consider it a sign of unfriendliness if he simply waves and continues on his way.

## Interrupting

In our fast-paced society, people who speak slowly often find themselves interrupted midway through a sentence, the trailing segment being correctly or incorrectly supplied by a zealous listener. Some speaking-impaired people do not mind being interrupted in this way; others call it the bane of their existence.

> I appreciate it if a person realizes that it's hard for me to talk and makes the effort to save me from speaking unnecessarily. If I'm saying something long and the person already understands halfway through, I'd like him to interrupt me.

> I have a co-worker at the fire station who always leaps in and finishes my sentences for me. It absolutely drives me up the wall. I realize I speak slowly, but it's so frustrating never to be able to finish what I'm saying.

> I go to a clinic where half the doctors have names beginning with M: Miller, Mahler, Mennell . . . Once I was calling for Dr. Mahler and I had trouble saying the name. The receptionist jumped in and started nervously reeling off all the names beginning with M, trying to guess which one I wanted. She was talking so fast I could hardly squeeze in, "No, it's — ." The whole episode would have gone so much more quickly if she'd just stopped a minute and waited for me to speak the name.

Our recommendation is as follows. Until you are familiar with a person's feelings on the matter, always allow him to finish what he is saying, even if he seems to be having a hard time saying it. Definitely, allow him to finish if you are not sure what he wants to say; do not make random guesses of what the end of his sentence might be.

## Surroundings for Listening

Although I've been deaf all my life, people tell me I speak quite well. When a person can't understand me, it is usually because of background noise. The situation improves dramatically when the radio or television is turned off.

For a person with a speaking impairment, a quiet place to talk is a haven. Noise interferes with conversation on two counts. First, it forces the speaker to raise his voice, often a difficult or impossible requirement. Second, it increases the likelihood that the listener will miss what is said and request a repeat performance.

It feels great when I've managed to get through an entire train of thought without stuttering. The most dreaded word in the English language is "huh?"

Many speaking-impaired people say that music is the most troublesome type of background noise. Others name television sets, car motors, and nearby competing conversations. As a rule, a noise that is similar in character to the person's voice has the greatest capacity to mask it out.

It's difficult if I'm on an airplane and other passengers try to start conversations, expecting me to speak. Planes are just too noisy, and I have my hands full doing the speaking that is essential to my travel. If I'm flying with friends or family, they know that this is their chance to get on a soapbox and talk all they want, uninterrupted. I'll be all ears!

Almost all people with speaking impairments prefer one-to-one conversations over group discussions. Groups are noisy, particularly if cross-conversations are taking place, and one must raise his voice to be heard. The conversation moves quickly, and the person who is slow on the draw is often left with mouth open and index finger poised as the discussion barrels along.

For speaking-impaired people, talking takes effort and concentration. Most say that talking while doing other things is not impossible but a lot harder than walking and chewing gum.

I use an artificial larynx so one hand is always occupied holding the device up to my throat when I'm talking. That limits what I can do while I talk. For example, in my sales job, I can't talk to customers while I'm using both hands to demonstrate a product.

When I have visitors, sometimes I have to go in the kitchen for a minute to check on the meal. It's such a nuisance if they come tagging after me, trying to chat. I can't cook and talk to someone at the same time. I usually try to be gracious about it, but what I really want to say is, "Buzz off until I'm finished!"

## Written Messages

For a person who is speaking impaired, writing messages down on paper is sometimes a workable alternative to speaking. It is slow, and cannot be done while walking down the street carrying two bags of groceries, but all in all it gets the job done.

If you are with a person who communicates by writing, refrain from initiating a conversation in a place where writing would be unusually awkward. The minimum requisites are a place to sit, a free hand, and some light. For an extended conversation, a table is also nice.

Understand that writing takes longer than speaking. Do not ask him a question if you do not have time to wait for an answer. And do not give him heartburn by asking a second and third question while he is still answering the first. Allow him to finish writing before you attempt to read the message.

If he is not hearing impaired, ask him if it is all right for you to keep talking while he is writing. Some people can write and listen at the same time, provided neither topic is unusually profound.

> It's fine with me if the other person talks while I'm writing. I've trained myself to be able to split my concentration in two. Although I must admit, occasionally I do get tripped up by doing that, and the message I write comes out strangely jumbled. The other person has to have a sense of humor!

If you cannot read his writing, speak up. He is probably trying to strike a balance between speed and legibility, to produce a message that is reasonably clearly written before you have nodded off. Let him know if he needs to slow down and tip the scales a notch toward legibility.

> Sometimes I write a very short message and the other person stares at it expressionless for an eternity. I start wondering whether he found my message unusually thought-provoking or he just can't read my hand-writing. I'm happy to slow down and write more clearly, if that's the problem.

Read the entire message before beginning to answer. The conversation will become too schizophrenic if you read a little at a time and then try to respond to each fragment.

If he is hearing impaired and you want to write a response, you may borrow his pen and paper. Otherwise, avoid borrowing these items; if you absolutely must, give them back afterwards!

> Without fail, seeing me with my pen and writing pad reminds my sister that she has to make out her grocery list. She always says, "You're not using these right now, I'll just borrow them," leaving me incommunicado for 15 or 20 minutes.

> People keep borrowing my pen and walking off with it. On a bad day I can lose 3 or 4 pens. Then the next time I want to say something to someone, I don't have a pen. The person I want to talk to probably thinks I'm a really ditsy person, to have a speaking disorder and not have the sense to carry a pen.

Writing messages does not work well in a group where everyone else is speaking. The topic of conversation generally moves along rapidly, and the person who is writing is forever contributing anachronisms to the ongoing discussion. The situation becomes truly hopeless if each member of the group reads the message individually and responds in his own time frame. If you are sitting near a person who is communicating by writing, you can help by offering to read his messages aloud to the others. When you do so, read word for word; do not confuse the listeners by intermingling your own comments. Also, take care to read it correctly so he will not have to release a new dispatch to amend the old one.

## High-Tech Messages

Writing messages longhand can be tedious. Some speaking-impaired people prefer instead to carry a typewriter, small computer, or similar device and use it for communicating with others. Since most people are able to type faster than they write, this kind of communication aid can save a lot of time.

Communication aids are not without drawbacks. Most are expensive, and they are more troublesome to lug around than a pencil and paper. Some communication aids also take a moment to turn on and set up, by which time one's audience may have thinned out.

> I need to put my keyboard down on something before I can begin typing. You'd be surprised how often no appropriate surface is available. I was trying to talk to my doctor's receptionist last week. Her desk was incredibly cluttered and there was no corner of it that I could easily commandeer.

A basic communication aid prints the message on a piece of paper or displays it on a screen. Snazzier versions broadcast the message by synthesized voice. With the current state of the art, the voice usually takes some getting used to.

> Once I came in late to class. When I turned on the device, it automatically said, "Hello," in its strange, mechanical voice. Everyone in the class looked around in bewilderment.

Perhaps the most exasperating aspect of using a fancy communication aid is the curiosity of others. Users cite the tedium of not being able to get a tank of gas or buy a quart of milk without stepping through a song-and-dance routine demonstrating their device. Worse yet is the anxiety of having an expensive and essential instrument handled by inexperienced fingers.

> The roller only holds a little paper, not enough to waste it. Also, the paper is more expensive than you might think.

> I don't want other people tinkering with it. They could break it. It would cause me great inconvenience to be without it, even for a while, because I also have an impairment which affects my arms and I cannot write well.

> It is especially frustrating being with computer professionals. They absolutely will not rest until they've seen and played with it for 20 minutes.

Many users of communication aids will gamely give a demonstration, but most draw the line at actually handing the device over. Our recommendation: do not even ask for permission to toy with it, so he will not have to play the heavy and turn you down.

# 23.

## SIGN LANGUAGE

Sign language, or "signing," is a method of communication which uses hand movements and positions to represent words or ideas. Many people with hearing impairments and a few with speaking impairments know and use it.

For a person who is communication impaired, the decision of whether or not to put the effort into learning sign language is a personal one.

I used to think all deaf people knew sign language. A week after I lost my hearing, still in a state of shock, I went to enroll in signing lessons. The instructor got out a pencil and said, "Is anyone in your family deaf?" I said, "No." And she said, "Do you know anyone who is deaf?" I said, "No." And she said, "Who are you going to sign to?" I had to admit, she had a point.

My vision isn't good enough for lipreading. Sign language is easier to see because the hand movements are a lot larger than lip movements.

When I ask people to write things down for me, they say, "Why don't you just learn to lipread?" I come from a deaf family, so I grew up with signing. Lipreading is a skill and an art, and like a lot of people, I'm just not very good at it.

Many communication-impaired people find sign language to be their most natural option. Sign language is easier to master than lipreading and speaking, especially for a person who has never heard speech. It is less demanding on the eyes than lipreading and calls for far less guesswork. It does not require particularly good lighting, a quiet environment, or a full frontal view. And it is a lot quicker than writing things down on paper. Unfortunately, all these advantages are countered by a single disadvantage: most people in the population at large do not understand it.

I was born deaf. I tried to learn to speak, but it was not a practical way for me to communicate. Forming the words correctly took so much concentration that I'd be worn out in five minutes. I'm lucky; a lot of people where I work know sign language, and of course my family does. I figure, when I'm with someone else, I'll just write.

111

Sign language has its own conventions of grammar; words and thoughts do not necessarily have the same sequence as in spoken or written English. Therefore, a person whose primary language is sign language may, when required to speak or write, use the English language in a manner that seems stilted. Some people have little opportunity to use English and do not speak or write it fluently.

Learning sign language is a time-consuming process which is probably not worth the effort for those who are not communication impaired and who have no occasion to use it on a regular basis. Fingerspelling is a different matter; after learning only 26 hand symbols, a person can communicate by manually spelling out words. Fingerspelling can be mastered in a few hours. It is a useful skill, especially for people who deal with the public in the course of their work.

A restaurant down the street has a couple of waiters who know finger-spelling and who always make us feel welcome. My friends and I often go there to eat, and we ask for those waiters. It's just so much easier and more pleasant than going someplace where we'll have to be guessing whether the waiter is saying "ranch dressing" or "french dressing."

# 24.

## INTERPRETERS

A professional interpreter can simplify conversation between a person who is communication impaired and one who is not. An interpreter has normal hearing and speaking abilities and also has a special communication skill. A "signing interpreter" is skilled in sign language. An "oral interpreter" silently forms words with her mouth, for a person who is hearing impaired and can lipread.

> I read lips well and have never learned sign language. But at business conferences I can't see everyone's face so I can't lipread. I usually bring an oral interpreter who sits by me and mouths what is being said.

Few communication-impaired people can afford the cost and inconvenience of having an interpreter in tow for everyday errands and social functions. Normally, an interpreter is used only in settings where accurate communication is vital, such as at a doctor's appointment, lawyer's office, or at a professional meeting.

> When I have no interpreter, I write back and forth to hearing people. Writing is slow, and I always feel like the information I get is limited. So I take an interpreter when the occasion is important and when I can afford it.

When you are communicating through an interpreter, things will go more smoothly if you observe a few conventions. Greet the interpreter when you first meet her; thereafter, direct all your dealings to the communication-impaired person, the person with whom you have business. Face this person and speak as though no interpreter were present. For example, say, "I have your papers ready," rather than, "Tell him that I have his papers ready." The interpreter will relay the words exactly as you say them.

> It really works best when the hearing person just pretends the interpreter is not there. At first it may seem rude to exclude a person in that way, but that's how it's done and that's what the interpreter expects.

113

While the interpreter is on duty, she is being paid to interpret verbatim everything that is said in her presence. Do not attempt to engage her in a side conversation, and do not say anything that you do not want interpreted!

> Most people don't realize that an interpreter interprets absolutely everything. Last week, I was in a man's office, and he answered a phone call. As he was talking, he casually glanced over and did a double take when he saw my interpreter interpreting what he was saying. If the man had not wanted me to hear the call, he should have asked me to step out, just as he would do if I were a hearing person.

Do not ask an interpreter for personal opinions or try to involve her in the business at hand. She cannot function effectively when asked to do things that are not part of her job.

> I sometimes find my lawyer asking the interpreter questions that he should be directing to me. I tell him that the interpreter is present to assist in our communications, not to make legal decisions for me.

If you are concerned about the privacy of your conversation, you may ask the interpreter to leave for a moment; then you and the communication-impaired person can converse in writing or some other manner. But this precaution is usually superfluous; it is the interpreter's obligation to hold in strict confidence anything she learns in the course of her work.

> If I have important business to conduct, I always use a certified interpreter. I don't worry about privacy. If an interpreter didn't keep my business private, he'd lose his certification. I know that, because I'm on the board which certifies interpreters!

Interpreting is a process that proceeds at about the same rate as spoken conversation, so speak at your normal speed. Do not attempt to ease the interpreter's burden by abbreviating what you want to say or leaving out information that you think would be hard to interpret. Doing that would defeat the purpose of having an interpreter.

Understand that, as with any translation process from one language to another, certain subtleties may not quite survive intact. Choose your words to be as clear and direct as possible. Avoid colloquialisms or other figures of speech. For example, say, "I'm tired," rather than, "I'm dead on my feet."

If several people are involved in the conversation, do not throw the interpreter into overdrive by speaking all at once. Only one message can be interpreted at a time.

For situations where privacy and accuracy are crucial, an interpreter who has been state or nationally certified will bring the highest standards of professionalism. In less critical settings, sometimes a friend, relative, or other person acts as an informal interpreter. Here, procedures are usually more relaxed. That person is probably participating in the conversation and cannot interpret as completely or accurately as would someone being employed to do nothing else.

> If I'm sitting with a group of friends and one of them knows sign language, often that person will interpret for me and save me from having to lipread. When that happens, I accept that this person can't interpret everything that is being said.

It is not uncommon for a hearing child to interpret for a communication-impaired parent or relative. When you are speaking to someone through a young interpreter, understand that the child is not equipped to handle complex or emotionally charged interchanges.

# 25.

## TELEPHONE

### The Telephone and Hearing Impairments

I have a volume control on my telephone, which is a big help. Still, talking on the phone is one of the most troublesome aspects of my hearing impairment. The sound is less clear than it is in person, and sometimes there is static on the line. On top of that, I don't have the advantage of being able to see lip movements or facial expressions.

Some hearing-impaired people have adequate partial hearing and speech skills to use the telephone. However, few have an overwhelming fondness for doing so. Those ascribing to the if-you-can't-beat-'em,-join-'em school of thought sometimes have special features incorporated into their telephone, to make its use more palatable.

I use a speaker (room amplifier) for the phone. I always have a hearing person present who can tell me what is said, then I can answer by myself. This method keeps me involved in the conversation.

Unless encouraged to do so, do not call a hearing-impaired person just to chat. Use the telephone for messages and save the serious socializing for face-to-face encounters.

When making your call, let the phone ring a little longer than you ordinarily would. The other person may not hear it immediately.

Before you begin to speak, try to calm the noise on your end of the line; turn down the TV, shut off the dishwasher, and try to strike a bargain with your shrieking kids. Collect your thoughts ahead of time so you can convey your information in a concise and straightforward manner.

Talk directly into the receiver, clearly and firmly. Speak moderately slowly and pause at the end of a sentence. If you have a foreign accent, be aware that you may be more difficult to understand over the telephone than in person.

I use my better ear on the telephone. Still, I have to ask the other person to repeat a lot of things. With a name, I usually have to ask him to spell it, which is embarrassing if it turns out to be Brown.

116

Since you do not have the option of supplementing your speech with writing or gesture, be prepared to spell, rephrase, or use more creative means of getting your point across.

Recently a friend used the word "tank" in a telephone conversation. I simply could not understand what she was saying, even when she spelled it. Finally, she said, "Do you remember history and General Sherman? Do you recall what they named for him?" Thanks to a wonderful history teacher I had 45 years ago, I understood immediately: the Sherman tank. A bit of frustration had turned to fun.

## The Telephone and Speaking Impairments

I like to do my telephoning early in the day, when I'm fresh and my voice is at its best. With just a little patience on the part of the other person, things usually go pretty smoothly.

There have been times when I've used a half a tank of gas to go see someone rather than having to call him. That's how much I dislike using the telephone.

Some people with speaking impairments avoid the telephone; they prefer face-to-face conversations, where speech can be augmented with facial expression, writing, and gesture. Others do not mind using the phone. Until you are familiar with his preference on the matter, call a speaking-impaired person only when you have a bona fide reason; do not phone him just to visit. Place your call at a time when you can give it your full attention so you will not have to ask him to repeat things unnecessarily.

Understand that the person you are calling may need to speak slowly, and that there may be pauses in his speech. These pauses may seem longer on the telephone than in person because you do not have the benefit of continued visual contact. If you hear an unexplained silence, either when you first call or during the conversation, be patient; do not hang up, humming the theme from *The Twilight Zone.*®

Time is something that I need a lot of. That is a problem on the phone because the other person can't see what's going on. My friends know that I stutter, that a long pause doesn't mean I'm dead. But people who don't know me sometimes are alarmed by a pause in the conversation. They get excited and say, "Hello, hello, hello, are you there?" which puts a lot of pressure on me.

I use a respirator to help me breathe, and I can only speak when the respirator is exhaling. In person, people see what is going on and understand the pauses in my speech, but over the phone they can't. Sometimes they hang up before I can even say, "Hello."

If you are having trouble understanding, ask him to repeat himself as soon as you realize you are waylaid. Do not remain silent, hoping to figure things out as you go along; chances are, you will not regain your orientation, and you will find it increasingly difficult to function as a credible party to the conversation.

Unless encouraged, keep the conversation of moderate length. If you hear volume or intelligibility beginning to slide, or if an increasing number of responses are monosyllabic, be aware that fatigue may be setting in; suggest that you converse more another time.

### Telecommunication Devices for the Deaf

A Telecommunication Device for the Deaf, or TDD, makes it possible to transmit typewritten information over the telephone. This device has a keyboard on which to type messages and a screen on which to view them. Both parties of the conversation must be using a TDD for the system to work. Many people with hearing or speaking impairments own and use a TDD.

> A lot of doctors' offices insist on having my phone number. I explain that I am deaf and cannot talk on the phone, and that if they need to reach me they'll have to use a TDD. Usually they don't understand what I'm talking about and just write my number in their files, which is pretty useless.

If you would like to call a person who has a TDD but you yourself do not have one, you can enlist the assistance of a special service to act as intermediary. This service, often called a "voice exchange" or "message relay service," is available in major cities. The voice exchange operator will speak and listen to you over one telephone line and communicate with the other person via TDD on another line. Speak slowly so the operator has time to type your message to the other party. Then be patient while the other person types his response and the operator reads it to you.

# 26.

## LENDING AID

One of the most troublesome aspects of my speech disorder is not being able to speak loudly enough to be understood on the telephone. At home I have a TDD, but when I'm on the road and late for an appointment, I can't whip over to a pay phone and call. When I'm lost, I can't phone ahead for directions. It can be a godsend to find someone to make a call for me.

I can use my phone at home because it's amplified, but I can't hear well on another phone. When I'm in public, sometimes I need help. At the library recently, the fan belt of my car broke and I needed to call a tow truck. I knew that the phone conversation would involve numbers and addresses and I didn't want any slip-ups, so I asked the nice garage attendant if he would please make the call.

You do not need to be a trained interpreter to assist a communication-impaired person with a conversation. Even with no special skills, you can be helpful, simply by virtue of being available when the need arises. The need for assistance frequently occurs with the telephone.

If you are asked to make a phone call by a hearing-impaired or speaking-impaired person, your major objective is to channel the message clearly and correctly in both directions, with a minimum of erosion in information. Be sure you understand ahead of time what needs to be accomplished by the call. If necessary, have the person write down key pieces of information, and then refer to these as you speak. For a complicated conversation, check with him one last time before you hang up, to be sure he has nothing to add. After you hang up, give him a complete explanation of what transpired. You need not repeat the entire dialogue verbatim if the information is not critical. But do hit all the high points; do not leave him hanging by winding up 15 minutes of exuberantly animated conversation and saying, "Your appointment is at three."

Occasionally, it might be useful for you to act as intermediary in a face-to-face encounter. For example, if you are a native speaker, you might be able to help a hearing-impaired person understand someone with a foreign accent. Or, you might help a speaking-impaired friend place his order in a noisy restaurant.

> Some people can't understand my speech at all. Others seem to do just fine. I'm not offended if the person I want to talk to doesn't understand and enlists the aid of someone nearby.

> When I take my car to be serviced, I know the garage will be noisy and I'll have trouble talking. It's so much easier if I have a friend with me who can talk to the mechanic.

Your services as intermediary may be especially appreciated when a communication-impaired person wants to speak with a child. Children's voices are higher pitched than those of adults, and hearing-impaired people generally have a hard time hearing them. Small children cannot communicate in writing, and often, they are unable to understand the speech of a speaking-impaired person.

> Every Christmas I play Santa Claus at the nearby hospital. I love doing this, but I cannot always hear the kids with their squeaky little voices. I have to say to the parent, "Mommy, would you write Santa a note about that?"

One of the most helpful things you can do for a hearing-impaired person is to provide him with information he might not otherwise obtain. Hearing-impaired people often miss what is said on loudspeakers, radios, and television sets because the sound is less clear than in person and because lipreading is difficult or impossible.

> When the Challenger accident occurred, everyone heard about it on the radio almost immediately. Although all the people at work know I am deaf and can't hear the radio, no one thought to tell me about it. I learned the devastating news hours later, by chance.

> In airports, the loudspeaker just sounds like static to me. I can tell when an announcement is being made, but I can't understand what is said. It's so nice when someone sitting near me notices my hearing aid and tells me about it, even if it wasn't important. It's always reassuring to know they didn't announce that my flight was just cancelled.

Absolutely, tell a hearing-impaired person about any sounds that herald danger, such as a honking horn on the street or a fire alarm in an office building. In addition, you might want to occasionally let him know about certain other non-speech sounds.

> I can't distinguish sounds anymore. I don't know what they are or where they're coming from. I might hear something and not know if it's

thunder or an overhead plane. It makes me feel a part of things if people tell me. I've opened the door and been surprised to see the rain, when everyone else heard it.

# 27.

## BUSINESS ETIQUETTE

### For Cashiers, Tellers, and Salespeople

When I hear someone's voice for the first time, I don't understand him as well as I do later, after I've had a chance to listen to him for a while. Going into banks, stores, or offices is difficult because I am constantly having to deal with unfamiliar voices. On top of that, the people don't speak up because they don't know I'm hard of hearing. I can't explain my disability to every single person I encounter.

For a person with a communication impairment, shopping or running errands presents a challenge. Most public places have noise which interferes with conversation. Transactions tend to be short, so others do not have a chance to learn to deal with the particular impairment. Frequently, time pressure is an additional onus; a person who cannot communicate rapidly is often confronted with a harried clerk in front of him and a line of restless shoppers behind.

I have to be on my toes when I go shopping. I know someone is going to come and say, "May I help you?" so I have to be alert and ready for that. Otherwise I might not hear him and he'll think I'm rude. When I pay, I know the clerk will say, "May I have your driver's license and credit card?" Afterwards, he'll say, "Have a nice day," or, "Your credit card has expired."

As a salesperson, cashier, or teller, you can take some measures to make the transaction go more smoothly for a customer who has a communication impairment. The first step is to recognize that an impairment exists. If you approach someone from behind, brightly offering assistance, and his gaze remains rivetted on the window display, that is a good clue that he has a hearing impairment. If someone steps up to your teller's window and hands you a note, consider that he may have a speaking impairment before you dive for the alarm button.

When I see a salesperson with an irritated look on his face, I suspect that he just asked me if he can help me and I didn't answer. I usually try to see a salesperson before he sees me. That way I can beat him to

122

the punch and say, "I'm just shopping around, thanks," before he can sneak up on me.

Take the time to listen carefully to what a speaking-impaired customer has to say. If you cannot understand him, ask him to repeat himself or invite him to write his message on paper. If he writes to you, find out whether he wants you to write also or to speak.

Be liberal with your explanations. Do not try to rush or abbreviate your communications when things are not going well.

> I'd like people to accept that I have to speak slowly. I always do business in places where the employees take the time to hear me out, where they make me feel like they value my patronage even though I have a speech disorder.

> In general, I just don't get enough information about the things I want to buy. I wish salespeople would have the patience to talk to me, repeat things, write things down if necessary. I have some hearing, and I can usually understand if they take an extra minute to explain.

Look at a hearing-impaired person whenever you speak to him. Do not try to talk to him while you are doing something else or walking around.

> The clerk at the post office always tries to talk to me while looking at the scale or punching numbers into the adding machine.

> The saleslady in the dress shop may go to the other side of the rack and keep talking.

> Cashiers talk to me while operating the cash register.

Understand that a person who is communication impaired may want less of your assistance than other customers. Past experience may have taught him that trying to explain his needs to you will take more time than simply serving himself.

Accept also that, for the sake of practicality, he may choose to forego the friendly small talk which often accompanies business transactions. Do not take it as a sign of aloofness if he plunges right into the business at hand, neglecting the customary confirmation that it is hot outside.

Avoid drawing undue attention to him and to the transaction. In particular, do not speak more loudly than is necessary while conducting his business; he will be gratified not to have curious onlookers apprised of his bank balance or pant size.

> People are not accustomed to the sound of my speech, which is deep pitched and very gravelly. They turn and look when I start to speak in

public, and this puts me under a lot of stress. Clerks sometimes make matters worse by shouting back to me. That's not necessary because my hearing is normal.

Write down numbers and important facts for a hearing-impaired customer, especially when it comes time to make a cash transaction. Remind him to take his change if it is delivered in a cup on the cash register; he may not be able to hear the coins descend.

## For Health Care Professionals

The possibility of imperfect communication is a way of life for people who have hearing or speaking impairments. Nowhere does this possibility cause greater concern than in a health care setting. As a health care professional, you can help ease the mind of a communication-impaired patient by showing a willingness to put some extra effort into communicating.

If a patient informs you that he has a communication impairment, relay that information to every member of the staff with whom he will have contact. In particular, prepare the staff if he will be communicating by writing. Your thoughtfulness will save him from having to explain his impairment to person after person during the course of his visit.

Let a hearing-impaired patient know that you will come get him in the waiting room when it is his time to be examined or served. Then he will not have to strain to hear each name being announced, watching the clock and wondering whether he has missed his turn.

> My ear doctor's office is the only place I can relax and read a magazine in the waiting room. There is a terrific nurse, and I know she won't let me miss my appointment. If I don't respond to my name on the loudspeaker, she always comes out to get me.

Emphatically, take whatever time is necessary to allow a speaking-impaired person to express himself. Be sure you have understood everything he wants to say before you take any action.

> Doctors and nurses tend not to give me enough time to explain things. My stuttering gets worse when they try to rush me.

> Since my laryngectomy, it's intimidating for me to go to a doctor. I know I won't be able to express myself as well as I used to, and I worry that if I don't get it right the first time, the doctor won't have the patience to hear me out.

Do not simplify or abbreviate explanations to a person who is hearing impaired. Understand that anything you have to say is of vital importance to the patient. Give complete information, and include some redundancy when you can. If there is any doubt in your mind that the patient has completely understood you, take the time to write down key facts.

I want to know anything that a hearing person would want to know. The other day I went to an eye doctor for a problem I was having. When he was finished examining me, all he said was, "Your eyes are good." That wasn't very satisfying to me. I want to know everything I can about my health.

Face a hearing-impaired patient any time you are speaking to him. Do not begin treating or examining him while you are talking.

It's very hard for me to lipread from a lying down position. When my dentist works on my teeth, I like her to tell me what she's going to do in advance, not after she has put the instruments in my mouth.

My gynecologist always tries to talk to me from behind the drape, which is disconcerting to say the least.

I have a wonderful eye doctor who really makes a special effort to make me feel comfortable. I cannot communicate in the dark so eye examinations are difficult. It takes a special doctor to have the patience to work around that problem.

Do not attempt to speak to a communication-impaired patient from another room. If the situation absolutely requires that you do this, get another person to stay in the room with the patient and act as intermediary.

In some hospitals, when you push the button for the nurse, she checks with you via the intercom before she comes in person. I have trouble raising my voice and speaking clearly on an intercom.

When I'm having an x-ray, the technician leaves the room and tells me when to hold my breath and when I can breathe again. Often I can't hear the instructions.

When a companion is accompanying the patient, be sure you understand her role. If she is a professional interpreter, speak directly to the patient as if the interpreter were not there; she will translate what you say verbatim. If she is a family member or interested party who is also facilitating communications, you may include her in the conversation. But resist the temptation to converse solely with her simply because it is easier to do so. Remember that it is the patient who must make informed decisions about his own health, and it is he who must understand and later comply with your instructions. Arriving at a complete meeting of minds between you and the companion accomplishes nothing!

Hand an adult patient his own prescriptions, bills, or other papers.

Most communication-impaired people place a high value on long-term relationships with health care professionals who understand and will accommodate their impairment. You can take a step toward building a good ongoing relationship by making an effort to remember or make note of the nature of the impairment; the patient will appreciate not having to start from scratch in explaining it the next time he sees you.

### For Restaurant Employees

Some waiters get rattled when I tell them I am deaf. Others take it in stride. There's a pizzeria that I like a lot. I can't think of anything special they do there, but they are always nice and helpful. They never act like my impairment is an insurmountable problem.

It does not take a major effort to make an establishment appealing and accommodating to a customer who is communication impaired. Half the battle is simply being aware of these impairments and being mentally prepared to deal with them.

If a customer informs you he has a hearing or speaking impairment, or if you observe that to be the case, come get him personally when it is his turn to be seated. Do not simply call his name or number; he may not hear you, or he may not be able to respond quickly or loudly enough to get your attention.

Seat him at a table away from the kitchen, in a quiet part of the restaurant. If possible, pick a spot that is also well lit, so he will be able to lipread or communicate by writing.

Be sure you have the attention of a hearing-impaired person before beginning to talk to him. Look directly at him and speak clearly. Stand in front of him so he will not have to break his neck turning around to read your lips. If he does not understand what you say, repeat yourself slowly, or spell a difficult word aloud. Forget about trying to deliver status reports, such as, "I'll be right with you," or, "Your food will be another minute," as you jog by his table. Either take the time to stop and make yourself understood, or skip it.

If the situation warrants it, write things down on paper. Do not shout, and do not do anything that would draw undue attention to the customer.

If you are in a position to do so, see to it that salad dressings, side dishes, drinks, and other offerings are all listed on the menu. This precaution will save you from having to figure out how to spell "roquefort" when the customer does not understand the spoken word. Post daily specials on a sign or write them on a card, to show to customers as necessary.

> Waitresses are so used to reeling off the same speech that it ends up all sounding like one word. Ask them what's for dessert, and they'll say, "Applepiepecanpiebrowniesandicecream."

> Once I was with a client at a restaurant, almost ready to leave, and the waiter came up and said something very hurriedly. I thought he was asking if our meal was all right, so I nodded "yes." Next thing I knew, here came another bottle of wine!

Listen carefully to a speaking-impaired person's order, and repeat it back if you are not sure you understood it correctly. Invite him to write if necessary. If he is ordering by pointing to items on the menu, read his selections aloud so he can confirm them.

> I can't speak loudly enough to be heard in noisy restaurants. Waiters need to have the patience to lean in closer and really listen, or else let me write. When they don't take the time to hear me out, I get coleslaw instead of coke, and we have to start over.

It may be his preference to have a companion place his order for him, but do not automatically assume that this will be the case. Speak to him directly unless you are requested to do otherwise.

Check back with the customer frequently to see if he needs anything. A person who is speaking impaired may not be able to talk loudly or clearly enough to get your attention. A hearing-impaired person may be unsure of how loudly to speak because he does not hear the background noise; he may be reluctant to risk bellowing out for you at the exact moment of a general letup in conversations.

Chances are, you converse with most of your customers more than is really necessary, and you could pare down your routine fairly easily. Some communication-impaired people would welcome that effort; others would not.

> Since it is so hard for me to talk, I am glad of every bit that I don't have to do. I love a waitress who just brings me a couple of kinds of steak sauce with my steak, instead of asking me if I want sauce and then asking me what kind.

> I want to be given the same service a hearing person would get. If

there's a choice, I want to know about it. I don't want to just get the default because it's too much trouble to talk to me.

Our recommendation is as follows. If you see a way to streamline communications without compromising his service, go ahead. But when in doubt, always ask and clarify. Remember that words are not the only way to communicate; do not skimp on the eye contact and friendly facial expression that make customers feel comfortable and welcome.

For a party of two or more, place the check in the middle of the table at the close of the meal. Do not assume someone other than the communication-impaired person will be paying the bill.

People with communication impairments are almost unanimous in naming their least favorite feature of eating out: drive-in microphones at fast food establishments. We suggest posting a sign stating that customers with hearing or speaking impairments may drive directly to the window. In the absence of such a sign, customers who take the liberty to bypass the microphone should be given the benefit of the doubt and spared the evil eye.

### For Public Transportation Officials

If you have a good story about the time you flew to Denver but your luggage ended up in Caracas, Venezuela, do not tell it in the presence of a communication-impaired person. He will very likely steal your thunder with a story about how his luggage erroneously went to Caracas and he went there with it!

Airports, taxi stands, train stations, and bus terminals are not settings conducive to good communications. The surroundings are noisy, and important information is often announced over poor quality loudspeakers. Officials and other passengers are generally in a hurry, so a person who does not understand or make himself understood the first time may not get a second chance.

I can't speak when I'm being jostled around on a bus, so I cannot ask the driver a question after we've started driving.

When I'm flying standby, I always worry that I won't hear my name being called and I'll be crossed off the list.

The situation is troublesome enough when events proceed without a hitch. But when there are cancellations, delays, or changes of schedule to contend with, a person with a hearing or speaking impairment is at a significant disadvantage.

> I was at a gate at the airport, ready to board, and all of a sudden everyone started walking away. The place of boarding had been changed, but I hadn't heard the announcement, and I had no idea what was happening.

> I often travel with my hearing dog. She will let me know if there is a fire alarm or other important sound. Airlines and buses are supposed to accommodate hearing dogs, just as they accept guide dogs for the blind. But sometimes, I run into an employee who isn't familiar with the policy and who denies me boarding. It can be extremely inconvenient. Hearing dogs are identified by their orange collar.

As a transportation official or employee, you can take certain actions to see that a communication-impaired passenger is properly served.

First and foremost, listen carefully to what the customer has to say. If you are not sure you have understood, repeat back key facts. Do not act on the information until you feel confident that communication has been complete.

> When I have to ask a bus driver about his route, I'm between a rock and a hard place. If I ask from the curb, I won't be able to hear his answer. But if I get on board, chances are he'll drive off before I'm sure I'm on the right bus.

Speak slowly and clearly, and take whatever time is necessary to ascertain that you have made yourself understood. If the situation warrants, write down important facts, such as gate numbers or departure times. The extra effort involved will be insignificant, relative to having to fly him back from Caracas.

> Cab drivers talk while they are driving, so I can't see their lips. Sometimes I tell them I am deaf and they just keep talking. I always hope they are not saying anything that will affect me.

A hearing-impaired person may not understand what is said over a loudspeaker; tell him anything important in person. Where possible, post relevant information in writing.

> I have never understood a single word a pilot has said over the speaker. He could be saying the plane is crashing and I wouldn't know it. I have found flight attendants to be very understanding of my situation. Once I tell them I am hard of hearing, they usually volunteer to keep me informed of anything I need to know. Then I can relax.

## Meetings and Classrooms

To help a hearing-impaired or speaking-impaired person make the most of a formal meeting, select a room with good acoustics and a minimum of extraneous noise. If you are in a position to do so, check with him ahead of time to see whether he would like an interpreter to help him understand and participate. If the answer is yes, find out what type of interpreter is required.

> A few years ago, before my hearing loss was as severe as it is now, I sometimes worked as a signing interpreter. Once I was hired to interpret for a deaf man at a legal proceeding. As I was signing, I was puzzled to see that the man wasn't really paying attention to me. I learned later that he was a lipreader and didn't know sign language. No one had even consulted him before hiring me!

If no interpreter will be present, take some extra measures to accommodate the communication-impaired person.

Offer him preferential seating, in a spot where he will have a good view of the speakers and where he will be able to participate without unduly raising his voice. Usually the best spot is in the front row of an audience or at the head of a rectangular table; on a panel, the best spot is near the center.

For a hearing-impaired participant, be sure the room is well lit. Adjust the volume of the microphone to give the clearest possible sound.

If you are the primary speaker, position yourself with the light on your face. Stay in one spot while you talk rather than pacing the floor. Stand so that your mouth is not directly behind the microphone.

Stop speaking when you turn to write on the chalkboard and do not resume until you can again face the audience; that way, the hearing-impaired person will not miss any of your lecture. When you refer to handouts or a textbook, allow a minute for your listeners to locate the proper material before you continue speaking.

For a long meeting, take an occasional breather. A person who is lipreading will appreciate the chance to rest his eyes for a moment.

Employ as many visual aids as possible. As the situation warrants, make liberal use of handouts, charts, or illustrations. Write down any new words or terms that you are introducing; it is almost impossible to lipread a word one has not previously encountered. Write down important facts, such as assignments or test dates. Do not rely on an oral announcement that all future meetings will be held in another building; the consequences of missing such a remark could be pivotal!

> Sometimes when I don't understand something in a meeting at work, I ask a friend about it later. There are times when I ask two different people the same question and get entirely different answers. It would be wonderful if they would use more handouts at meetings, so I could be sure of getting the right information.

Repeat all comments or questions from other people in the room before you respond to them. In particular, repeat comments from speaking-impaired people, for the benefit of those who are hearing impaired and others who may have trouble understanding.

Make occasional eye contact with a speaking-impaired person, to see if he has anything to contribute to the discussion. He may want to participate but not be able to speak up quickly at a momentary lull, if others are talking in rapid succession.

If you are sitting next to a hearing-impaired person in a meeting, the most helpful thing you can do is to be as quiet as possible. Hearing aids are sometimes sensitive to nearby extraneous noise, and if his is turned up to hear the speaker, your sipping of coffee could be sounding like fingernails on a chalkboard. Do not whisper to him; the interruption could make him lose the train of the speaker's narrative, and very likely he cannot understand whispers anyway. Use pen and paper if you must communicate with him during the meeting.

> I go to a lot of professional conferences, and people just aren't very quiet. I can't hear the speaker over all the shuffling of feet and clinking of ice water. It's especially hard when people sitting next to me try to engage me in little side conversations during the presentations.

Allow him to look at any notes you might be taking, and offer to fill him in afterwards on any points he may have missed. For a person who has a speaking impairment, particularly one who is not able to speak loudly, offer to ask questions for him during the meeting.

> It's easy to lose track in church services. It helps if a neighbor lets me peek at his prayer book to see where we are.

> I have a very special colleague who always makes an effort to sit by me at lectures. Then when the topic changes or a new term is introduced, she writes a couple of key words down on a piece of paper for me. I've never asked her to do this, she does it on her own. I appreciate it more than I can say.

# 28.

## INTRODUCTIONS

My hearing impairment complicates introductions. When I'm meeting a new person, my first hurdle is to catch his name, which may be difficult or unusual. Then I have to quickly attune myself to the way he speaks so I'll be able to understand him. All this without missing out on any of the conversation. I'm sure I sometimes seem a little dazed!

In informal settings, introductions are often passed over lightly; a simple "John, Jerry, Jerry, John" is considered ample. When you are introducing a person who is communication impaired, a less skeletal rendering is in order.

If possible, select a spot that is quiet. Then, introduce him to one or two people at a time rather than an entire group. Cross-indexing a battery of names with a row of smiling faces is a feat even if one is not communication impaired.

Pronounce names slowly and distinctly. A name is particularly difficult to hear and lipread because, unlike a regular word, it cannot be inferred from its context in a sentence.

After the introduction, stay a moment and help get the conversation started. Tell the people involved a little about each other.

When I meet someone, I know he or she is going to start asking where I live, where I work, and a dozen other questions. That means a lot of talking for me! It's nice if the person making the introduction supplies some of this information so I won't have to say it all.

People may not understand me at first, but if they hang in there a minute and listen, they usually start catching on. It helps if the person doing the introduction lingers on and chats for a few minutes while the other people get used to the way I speak.

If you think the person might have a difficult time explaining his own impairment, step in and do so for him. For example, if the surroundings are noisy and he speaks with limited volume, explain the situation to the other person. But if there is no obvious reason for you to intervene, let him decide how much, if anything, to say about his impairment.

I saw a man being introduced to my sister, who is also deaf. He started talking to her when she wasn't looking at him, and he appeared very hurt and insulted when she did not respond. I don't want to be in the position of offending someone before I've had a chance to tell him I am deaf. I want the person introducing me to explain that I cannot hear and will be lipreading.

Just introduce me as a human being, don't mention my impairment. It will be obvious when I start speaking and doesn't really need any explanation.

I want people to know why I'm not speaking, but I don't especially want to be introduced as Carol-with-the-voice-disorder. Last month at a small party, I thought the host handled it well. He waited until after all the introductions had been made and things had settled down, then he mentioned to the other guests that I had a speaking disorder and wouldn't be talking very much.

# 29.

## ENTERTAINING

When extending an invitation to a person who has a communication impairment, tell him enough about the occasion so he can judge whether or not he would enjoy participating. Be descriptive; facts that you normally consider unimportant may carry considerable weight with him. Explain where the event will be held, who will be there, and what kinds of activities are planned.

> I do best in quiet surroundings because I can't speak loudly. I would enjoy a party that maybe had music and dancing in one area and a quiet place for talking somewhere else. I probably wouldn't go to an occasion that was going to be one big stand-up-and-scream.

> I like to find out who is going to be there before I go. I especially enjoy doing things where I know most of the people so I can relax and don't have to keep explaining why my voice sounds unusual.

> Sign language is my major method of communication. Most likely, I wouldn't go to a get-together if no one was going to be there who knew signing.

One of the most important things you can do to help a communication-impaired person enjoy a social occasion is to keep background noise to a minimum. Do not run noisy appliances, turn music off or to a moderate volume, and avoid unnecessary commotion. For a guest who is hearing impaired, do not dim the lights. Stand near him when you make a general announcement, such as that the party is moving into the dining room, so he will not have to speculate on why people are suddenly filing out the door.

If a meal is being served, ask him if he has any special preference regarding where to sit at the table.

> I like to sit at the left end of a dining table so the conversation is in my better ear.

> I can't project my voice, so I like to sit near the center of the table where people can hear me.

Accept that he may not participate in the conversation to the same degree as the other guests. Follow his lead; if he is reticent for a period, do not make any unusual effort to draw him into the conversation or make him the center of attention. Do not ask him a chain of questions, request that he read aloud, or draft him to say grace. However, let him know by your friendly manner and occasional eye contact that his participation would be welcome.

> It's hard for me to carry on a conversation while I eat because I have to watch people's lips. If someone is asking me question after question, I never get any food! I try to sneak in bites, but everyone else finishes eating way ahead of me, and I never have a chance to enjoy my meal.

> I feel very much on the spot when a host asks me questions at the table in front of everybody. I prefer to talk to people one or two at a time, where I can relax and not have to raise my voice.

For an overnight guest who is hearing impaired, find out how he would like to be awakened in the morning. For example, he might want you to come touch his arm, or he may prefer that you flash the lights in his room on and off a few times.

> The biggest problem with overnight stays is getting up in the morning. I can't hear a regular alarm. At home, I use a clock radio that is set to the very loudest setting, and my husband has a heart attack every single morning. I would hate to do that to a host!

If he is alone in a room during the course of his stay, flash the lights when you enter. He may not hear your footsteps and lose ten years' growth when you tap him on the shoulder.

# 30.

## CONVERSATION

I lost my hearing very suddenly. If that had happened to somebody else, I'd be interested to know what had caused it and how he was managing. So I don't mind at all if other people want to know about me.

After I injured my voice, as I was seeing all the people who knew me before, everyone wanted to know what had happened. It was a litany, and I did not always want to use what little voice I had repeating it over and over.

My voice sounds like a loud whisper because I have one paralyzed vocal cord. I don't like it when total strangers bluntly say to me, "My God! What happened to your voice?" Nobody would go up to a bald guy and say, "My God! What happened to your hair?"

Others are often curious about an impairment; they wonder when and how it occurred or how it affects daily life. Some communication-impaired people welcome the interest and do not mind answering questions on the topic. In contrast, some prefer not to make repeated explanations to the idly curious. Usually this preference does not stem from any desire to be clandestine; certain impairments simply do not lend themselves to concise commentary.

When repair or delivery people come to the door, I tell them right away that I'm deaf. Without fail, they look quizzically at the doorbell, wondering how I heard it. Sometimes they're hesitant to ask, but I don't at all mind explaining the matter: my doorbell is hooked to a flashing light inside.

Sometimes, communication-impaired people enjoy jokes or lighthearted comments about their impairment; just as often, they do not. When a joke falls flat, it is usually because the comedian spoke before he understood the nature of the impairment. Witticisms from strangers and casual acquaintances are at greatest risk of descending like lead balloons.

I have an answering machine on my phone. Sometimes people call and hear stuttering on the tape and think it's a joke and stutter in the message they leave. It gets boring.

136

Although humor can misfire, we definitely do not recommend avoiding it altogether. Humor can be a delight to all when offered by a friend, in the spirit of sharing and fraternity.

I have friends who tease me a little about my voice, but they do it in a loving manner. The other day at a restaurant, I had a lot of trouble saying the word "chili" to the waitress. After she left, my friend said, "Glad you didn't order fettucini Alfredo, we might have been here until dawn."

My assistant's husband was going to take me to lunch one day, shortly after I lost my hearing. When he pulled up in front of the building, instead of honking the horn as usual, he stood outside the car and held up a big sign that said, "Honk, honk." I loved it!

## Outwitted

*He drew a circle that shut me out—*
*Heretic, rebel, a thing to flout.*
*But Love and I had the wit to win:*
*We drew a circle that took him in!*

Edwin Markham

# INDEX

## A

Access (*see* Architectural barriers)
Activity, social (*see* Social event)
Aid (*see* Help)
Aisles, wheelchairs and, 24, 28
Appliances, mobility impairment and, 5, 8,
    9, 22, 26, 29, 35, 36 (*see also* Wheelchair,
    Wheelchair user, Canes, Crutches,
    Walker)
Architectural barriers,
    definition of, 14–15
    private homes and, 18, 34–35, 40
    public places and, 18, 23, 27, 28,
        29–30
    (*see also* specific barriers such as Doors,
        Stairs, Rest rooms)
Arrival,
    mobility-impaired person's, 28, 34–35, 38
    visually impaired person's, 60, 66, 74,
        81–83
Assistance (*see* Help)
Attention,
    getting a hearing-impaired person's, 95
    getting a visually impaired person's, 74
Audiotape, 62, 68, 72, 74

## B

Barrier (*see* Architectural barriers)
Bathroom (*see* Rest rooms)
Books (*see* Written materials)
Braille, 61, 68, 71, 72
Buffet, 27, 67, 68, 80
Bus drivers, 70–71, 129
Bus stops, visually impaired person and, 70
Business card (*see* Written materials)
Business etiquette, 23–30, 63–72,
    122–131

## C

Canes,
    mobility-impaired person and, 9, 26, 35,
        36, 38
    visually impaired person and, 47, 51,
        56–58
Car (*see* Vehicle)
Carrying mobility-impaired person, 15, 34
Cashiers, 24, 25–26, 63–64, 122–124
Chairs,
    mobility-impaired person and, 26, 28, 35,
        38, 40
    visually impaired person and, 66, 67, 79,
        81, 85
Children, 42–43, 88, 120
Classrooms, 130–131
Communicating in writing (*see* Writing)
Communication aids for speaking-impaired
    person, 109–110
Communication impairment, definition of,
    92
Communication, methods of, 93–94
Conversation,
    initiating, 38, 73, 94
    position for, 31, 96–97
    topics of, 74–76, 32–33, 136–137
    (*see also* Curiosity, Empathy,
        Introduction, Humor, Personal
        appearance, Private topics)
Conversations, group,
    hearing-impaired person and, 102–103
    speaking-impaired person and, 107, 109
Counters in places of business, 25
Crutches, 24, 25, 26, 35, 36
Curb service, 24, 25
Curbs, 12, 15, 54 (*see also* Stairs)
Curiosity, 32, 42–43, 88, 136 (*see also* Private
    topics)

139